Dyslexia in the Workplace

Dyslexia in the Workplace

DIANA BARTLETT BSc(ECON), BSc(PSYCHOL)
Tuition for Dyslexic Adults, London

and

SYLVIA MOODY PHD, C PSYCHOL
Dyslexia Assessment Service, London

Consultant in Dyslexia:
PROFESSOR MARGARET SNOWLING
University of York

W
WHURR PUBLISHERS
LONDON AND PHILADELPHIA

© 2000 Whurr Publishers
First published 2000 by
Whurr Publishers Ltd
19b Compton Terrace, London N1 2UN, England and
325 Chestnut Street, Philadelphia PA 1906, USA

British Library Cataloguing in Publication Data
A catalogue record for this book is available from the
British Library.

ISBN: 1 86156 172 5

Printed and bound in the UK by Athenaeum Press Ltd,
Gateshead, Tyne & Wear

Contents

Foreword

If you have picked this book up wondering whether it is a book for professionals who deal with issues related to dyslexia or for people who are dyslexic, the answer is YES in both cases: this book will be of great interest to both categories of readers. (I can also imagine a few Smart Alecs thinking 'If they're dyslexic they won't be able to read the book' - you really need to read this book!)

Understanding the impact of dyslexia in the workplace is both important and challenging. It is important because, as illustrated in the following chapters, dyslexia can have a massive adverse effect on people's employment prospects and achievements. It is also an area where suitable help can make a great deal of difference. The challenge is for all of us, not least people with dyslexia, to be creative in finding solutions and valuing the strengths that are often associated with dyslexia.

Dyslexia in the Workplace is a very welcome addition to the small number of publications that deal with the interface between dyslexia and employment. The numerous examples in this book give vivid illustrations of the nature of the problems and the commentary is well researched without being obscure or excessively academic. I am particularly pleased that there is a chapter on dyspraxia. It helps to emphasize that there is a vast range of manifestations of 'specific learning difficulties'. The challenge which Diana Bartlett and Sylvia Moody help us to understand, is to make sense of the special circumstances while still treating people as individuals, rather than falling into the trap of making assumptions that dyslexics cannot do x, y and z.

Doubtless I have been invited to write this foreword because of my involvement in trying to improve employment services for people with dyslexia. However, this is a personal endorsement of the book rather than some official response. I only wish it had been around when I started thinking 'how could we do a better job in helping people with specific learning difficulties?' On that basis, I wholeheartedly commend this book to readers who are involved in selection, recruitment, vocational guidance, training and more generally concerned with encouraging people to turn their potential into achievement in employment.

Tim Edmonds
Employment Service,
Occupational Psychology Division.
June 2000

Preface

The problems faced by dyslexic children and students are now widely acknowledged and understood. However, there is often a lack of understanding of the problems experienced by working people who have dyslexic difficulties, for example the telephone engineer who has to fill in work records, the accounts clerk who constantly makes errors with numbers, or the manager who has to produce written reports.

In this book, the nature, assessment and management of dyslexic difficulties are discussed in a workplace context. In Part 1 of the book, the difficulties and the particular ways in which they manifest themselves in working life are described, and information is given about various forms of assessment. Some shorter chapters are included, which attempt to convey the experiences of dyslexic people in an immediate way. In Part 2, strategies for managing dyslexic difficulties are suggested. In Part 3, there is a review of recent research, a guide to the Disability Discrimination Act, and information about organizations that can offer help.

All the information given in this book will also be relevant to people who have dyspraxic difficulties. The terms 'dyslexia' and 'dyspraxia' have precise medical definitions, but in an educational context they are generally used in a rather loose way to refer to largely overlapping sets of specific learning difficulties; the difference between them is one of emphasis, dyslexia being associated chiefly with poor verbal memory and phonological skills, dyspraxia with poor perceptual processing and motor co-ordination.

It is useful to note, too, that dyslexia and dyspraxia are on a continuum not only with each other but also with 'normal' difficulties and inefficiencies. Almost any member of the population might feel that they had some area of inefficiency, perhaps in spelling or memory, or in telling left from right. What distinguishes the dyslexic/dyspraxic person from the 'normally inefficient' person is the extent and severity of the difficulties.

It is hoped, then, that this book will be useful to people with dyslexic/dyspraxic difficulties at all levels of responsibility in the workplace, to their employers and colleagues, and to those who are seeking work.

For clarity, throughout this book, we have referred to the dyslexic person as 'he' and to the professional concerned with helping him (psychologist, tutor, etc.) as 'she'.

We gratefully acknowledge help and comments on the manuscript from: Mary Colley, Tim Edmonds, Angela Fawcett, Alison Gallagher, Melanie Jameson, Katherine Kindersley, Chris Singleton, Martin Turner and Ann Wilson.

Part 1

Dyslexic difficulties and their assessment

Introduction

The first chapter in Part One covers the general nature of dyslexic difficulties and the specific ways in which these difficulties manifest themselves in the workplace. The next four chapters are devoted to assessment. In Chapter 2, the general principles of assessment are considered, and in Chapter 4, specific tests are described and reviewed. Two shorter chapters give advice on arranging an assessment and consider the emotions that can be stirred up by the assessment process. Dyspraxic difficulties are considered in Chapter 5, and in the final chapter in this part, dyslexic adults speak for themselves about their emotional reactions to their difficulties.

To begin with, however, may we introduce Mr Smith...

A GOOD DAY
AT THE
OFFICE?

In which we shadow Mr Smith, a
dyslexic clerk, during his working day.

Eight o'clock on Monday morning and Mr Smith leaves home as usual to catch the 8.30 train to Victoria. Alas, on reaching the station, he realizes that he has forgotten some important papers and has to return home to collect them. Consequently, he misses his usual train and arrives late at work, thereby incurring a reprimand from his boss and black looks from one or two colleagues who suspect him of shirking.

Mr Smith starts to sort through the pile of letters in his in-tray, but then suddenly remembers that he has an urgent report to write. He switches his attention to this, but after two hours of struggle, he is completely dissatisfied with his efforts. It doesn't help that he is interrupted by a telephone call from an irate client, who complains that Mr Smith has forgotten to send him some vital information. Mr Smith takes down the client's telephone number and promises to call him back with the relevant information in the afternoon.

At lunchtime, Mr Smith has a drink with his colleagues, who make what he feels to be snide remarks about his attitude to work; he withdraws into a sulky silence and returns early to the office.

Back at his desk, he tries to telephone the irate client who had called earlier but finds that he has written down the man's telephone number incorrectly. He tries to locate the client's file only to discover that he has somehow misplaced it.

He decides to make a further effort with the report he is trying to write but then suddenly remembers that he is due at a meeting in a nearby building at 2 o'clock. He looks at his watch: 2.30! He snatches up a file and races to the meeting venue. Although he has been given clear directions on the telephone, he gets completely lost and arrives at the meeting an hour late. Not only that but he then realizes that he has brought the wrong file with him.

Back at the office again he tries to write a memo about the meeting he has just attended, but finds it hard to recall exactly what was said. In the meantime, his boss, who has been looking through Mr Smith's efforts at report writing, summons him to complain that what he has written is incomprehensible. He also fulminates about a recent expenses claim put in by Mr Smith, who, owing to a careless clerical error, has claimed £10 000 for a weekend conference in Brighton.

Disheartened, indeed close to despair, Mr Smith spends the rest of the afternoon staring at the wall. At 5.30 he leaves the office to catch his train home from Victoria. He discovers that his usual train has been cancelled. It seems like the only event of the day that is not his fault.

He arrives home an hour late to be greeted by his wife in traditional fashion with a kiss and the question: 'Did you have a good day at the office, dear?'

Chapter 1
Dyslexic difficulties in the workplace

A review of various aspects of dyslexic difficulties and the way they affect efficiency at work.

Overview

Dyslexic difficulties can make a day at the office an ordeal, if not a nightmare. One reason is that the difficulties are various and not always easy to define or pinpoint. The term 'dyslexia' has borne a number of meanings over the years. Originally it was used to mean difficulty with reading, and in a medical context it still means precisely this. In the educational world, however, it is used more loosely to cover difficulty not only with reading but also with spelling, writing and mathematics; it may also denote a range of general difficulties associated with weak short-term memory, poor phonological processing ability, and inefficient hand–eye skills.

A dyslexic person, therefore, may have difficulty not just with reading and writing, but also with remembering instructions, addresses and appointments; he may find it difficult to copy accurately, to file things in the correct order, to read maps, and to distinguish left from right; he may operate generally in a state of muddle and confusion; and, unlike the true incompetent, he is likely to feel that, somewhere in the midst of this chaos, there is an able person trying to get out.

An economical way of describing the manifold difficulties of a dyslexic person is to say that he takes a long time to process information. Thus, he can easily feel overwhelmed by incoming information, whether this reaches him in the form of the written or the spoken word; hence he balks at having to digest long reports and tends to lose the thread of discussions. He has difficulty, too, in transmitting information clearly and succinctly to the outside world in speech or writing; he knows what he wants to say but easily gets muddled, especially if he has to say – or write – it in a hurry.

A concrete analogy would be a clerk sitting at his desk trying to concentrate on his work – work that he is quite competent to do. He is continually distracted, however, by a succession of post-boys, who approach his desk every few minutes hurling piles of urgent files into his in-tray and demanding his outgoing letters. This gives some idea of the experience of a dyslexic person: he feels so overwhelmed by the volume of incoming and outgoing information that he loses his capacity to work calmly and efficiently.

This bewildering mix of competence and inefficiency may make the dyslexic a difficult employee. He is not easy to 'place'. He seems discontented with a subordinate position and eager for a greater challenge, but his inefficient ways constantly act as a barrier to promotion.

Some dyslexics, it is true, have risen to important positions. These are often the ones who have perfected the art of concealment – or perhaps they have been blessed with literate secretaries or spouses. One way or another they have muddled through – but usually at a price.

When asked how they feel about their difficulties, adult dyslexics use such words as: angry, frustrated, embarrassed, ashamed, humiliated, panic-stricken. No one likes to feel they are making a fool of themselves and the emotional reactions to dyslexic difficulties make these very difficulties worse. Feelings of shame and embarrassment have prompted some dyslexics to take dramatic action which they have later regretted: they have flounced out of meetings, refused to meet clients, even given in their notice.

But there is a constructive alternative. Dyslexic difficulties can be alleviated, managed and accommodated in the workplace. The first essential step is recognize them for what they are. In practice, they often go unrecognized because dyslexia is still often regarded as principally a reading difficulty, though many adult dyslexics have, by dint of hard work and determination, learned to read with reasonable competence; it is the writing, memory and organizational skills that remain a major handicap.

In the next section, we consider some of the factors that underlie dyslexic difficulties; and then we go on to look in more detail at how efficiency in the workplace is affected.

Underlying difficulties

Some brief general remarks are made here about four areas in which the dyslexic person may be weak: phonological processing, short-term memory, sequencing, and hand–eye skills; and ways in which such weaknesses affect general literacy skills are noted. (For more details of the relevant research, see Chapter 19).

Phonological processing skills include, for example, awareness of the phonological segments of spoken words, the ability to map directly from letters to sounds in reading, and the ability to spell words by ear. When dyslexic adults who appear to have achieved reasonable competence in reading and writing are given tests that tap 'pure' phonological ability (such as reading non-words, producing spoonerisms), they typically perform worse than their non-dyslexic peers, particularly in respect to speed.

Short-term memory is the memory we use to store information that we need to keep in our minds for a brief time, for example, the telephone number we are about to call. If, rather than just passively storing information, we want to use the stored information in some way, then our short-term memory becomes a 'working memory'; thus we use working memory for tasks such as doing mental arithmetic or saying numbers backwards.

It has been proposed that one component of working memory is a 'phonological store', a deficit in which will result in difficulties with the immediate recall of phonological material. Such a deficit could also hinder the transfer of phonological information into long-term memory, thereby making it difficult for us to remember letter–sound correspondences or to acquire an extensive vocabulary.

Sequencing is a skill which is involved in many cognitive tasks, but it is particularly crucial in reading and writing. It is needed, for example, in the visual analysis of the letters in a word and in the ordering of the sounds of those letters. It is important, too, in reading and understanding extended text: the sequence of words in a sentence, the sequence of sentences in a paragraph and the general line of thought of the writer all need to be followed. Aspects of sequencing ability such as these may, perhaps, equally well be termed serial short-term memory, but it should be noted that dyslexia seems to involve a general difficulty with sequencing tasks, irrespective of whether or not short-term memory is involved. For example, a dyslexic person may find it difficult to place a series of pictures in order to tell a story, even though he is not required to memorize the pictures.

Hand–eye skills (also called visuo-motor or perceptual/motor skills) are used in such tasks as writing and copying, distinguishing left from right, orienting oneself in space and analysing visual stimuli. A person with poor visuo-motor skills will tend to make reversal errors (p, q; b, d), will find it hard to keep his place when reading a text and may miss out words; in writing, he will find it hard to plan and structure his work, and to set things out neatly.

Specific workplace difficulties

The underlying difficulties in the four areas described above – phonological processing, memory, sequencing and hand–eye skills – cause
inefficiencies not just in literacy skills, but in every area of life in which
cognitive processes are involved. In this section we look in more detail at
areas of inefficiency in the workplace. For convenience, the difficulties
have been grouped under general headings though, in practice, there is
considerable overlap between the groups.

Reading

A dyslexic person who has achieved reasonable competence in reading
may manage perfectly well with everyday reading activities, such as
reading newspapers, magazines or letters. However, he may find work
tasks more arduous. Problems arise when he has to deal with large
amounts of written material, such as digesting a written report or the
contents of a thick file of information. When engaged on such tasks, the
dyslexic person tires much more quickly than his non-dyslexic counter-
part; tiredness quickly compounds his basic difficulties and further
reduces his efficiency.

He may also encounter difficulty even with a relatively short text if he
has to extract a detailed and precise meaning. Thus, he might find it hard
to follow detailed written instructions, for example, technical manuals or
protocols about work procedures. He will also have difficulty in reading
out loud, and so may feel uneasy if he has to read out reports at a
meeting or give a paper at a conference.

Writing

A dyslexic person may have difficulty with everyday writing tasks, such as
writing letters, and get in a muddle even with short written communica-
tions, such as memos, notes to colleagues or reports of telephone
messages. He may have trouble filling in forms or worksheets; and he will
certainly be daunted when confronted with tasks in which a great volume
of writing is required, for example, preparing reports. He will have difficulty not just with the 'nuts and bolts' of writing (spelling, punctuation,
grammar, sentence structure) but will find it hard to organize his ideas
when preparing a piece of written work, and to express himself in a clear,
logical and succinct way. Often he writes in a style that is an awkward
mixture of jargon and colloquialisms ('Consideration is currently being
given to representations submitted by the operatives that they want more
time for tea').

Numbers

The dyslexic person will find numbers difficult in a variety of ways. First, he may make reversal errors (6, 9,); second, he may make sequencing errors (2423, 2432); third, he will find it difficult to keep numbers in their correct columns:

$$\begin{array}{r} 96 \\ 230 \\ \hline 1190 \end{array}$$

Further, he may have a general difficulty in understanding mathematical concepts, such as percentages, and remembering the correct procedures to calculate these. He may be poor at estimating relative magnitude and fail to notice that his calculations have produced implausible answers. For example, he might calculate 15% of £80 to be £35, and not immediately see that this answer must be wrong.

Short-term memory

Short-term memory is an indispensable tool in most everyday tasks, indeed in most human activities. Some examples of it in use in working life would be: a car mechanic reading a section of a technical manual and then applying what he has just read to the repair task he has in hand; an artist observing a model and then proceeding to draw what he has seen; a secretary taking down a telephone number; a lecturer listening to a question from his audience and formulating his answer to it; a waitress remembering an order long enough to write it down.

Inefficiencies caused by poor short-term memory are indeed myriad. Among those most commonly reported by working people are difficulty in:

- remembering telephone numbers
- remembering messages, instructions and directions
- following conversations, debates or lectures
- formulating one's thoughts when speaking to others
- recalling what was said at meetings
- concentrating for long periods
- multi-tasking (carrying out several mental operations simultaneously, for example, listening + taking notes + formulating a reply).

Sequencing abilities

Poor sequencing ability makes it hard for a dyslexic person to file documents in the correct sequence, to look up entries in dictionaries or directories, to carry out instructions in the correct order, to follow work protocols and to organize work schedules.

Organizational skills

Poor memory and sequencing ability appear to be linked to poor organizational skills. Dyslexics are often poorly organized in all areas of their life; at work they are notorious for missing appointments, getting the times and places of meetings wrong, failing to meet deadlines. They often live and work in a muddled, or even chaotic, fashion, always having their desks in a mess, constantly losing things and never having the right papers with them.

Visual orientation

A dyslexic person commonly has a tendency to confuse left and right, and more generally may find it hard to orient himself in space. He may find it difficult to digest information that is presented in the form of graphs, charts or columns of figures. He may easily get lost in strange surroundings and may lose his bearings even in a familiar place, such as a large office complex; if his job involves driving, he may struggle to read maps and be hampered by a poor sense of direction.

Hand–eye co-ordination

Poor hand–eye co-ordination can result in slow and untidy handwriting, poor presentation of written work or figures, and inaccurate keying on a word processor, calculator or telephone. In manual work it can manifest itself in general clumsiness or slowness in performing tasks. Usually, a dyslexic person has to make a trade-off between speed and accuracy, so that he is constantly in trouble either for not finishing his work or for making careless errors.

Speech

Perhaps because they feel largely 'locked out' of the world of the written word, and cannot easily 'discharge' their thoughts in writing, many dyslexics become voluble talkers – though they often feel that they talk in an over-elaborate and disorganized way, especially when they arc under pressure. By contrast, other dyslexic people feel so self-conscious about what they perceive as their inability to express themselves clearly in speech that they become hesitant and withdrawn, perhaps tending to respond briefly to what is said to them rather than holding forth themselves. If they are able to overcome their nervousness about speaking in public, they may have little difficulty in presenting material they have previously prepared (for example, a paper at a seminar), but they will be less able to make spontaneous contributions in seminars or meetings, and may feel great frustration about this.

Emotional reactions

The dyslexic person has to deal not only with his own frustration about his various inefficiencies, but also with other people's lack of understanding of, and respect for, his difficulties. As a result, he is likely to feel a mixture of unpleasant emotions – despair, anger, embarrassment, anxiety, lack of confidence – and may sometimes then behave in an aloof, defensive or aggressive way. (The emotional components of dyslexic difficulties are considered further in Chapters 7 and 16.)

Positive aspects of dyslexic difficulties

There is no pain without gain. Dyslexic people who try to succeed in their work despite their difficulties know the meaning of hard work, long hours and determination. They have a 'grit' which earns the respect of any employer who has some understanding of dyslexia. Further, the very fact that they are not quite in the general mould of analytical thinking may mean that they develop other, more holistic, ways of dealing with workplace tasks. Many dyslexics excel, for instance, in lateral thinking; they are creative and innovative, and are aware of links and associations that may escape the more linear thinker; they often have good powers of visualization, excellent spatial and practical skills, and an untaught intuitive understanding of how systems work. As one writer (West, 1991) has observed, they may struggle to keep up with their peers in the world of academic learning, but they have a natural wisdom!

Further reading

Reid G, Kirk J (2000) Dyslexia in Adults: employment and education. Chichester: John Wiley.

Chapter 2
Assessment: general considerations

An overview of the general principles governing the assessment of dyslexia, and the types of assessment available. (Specific tests are described in Chapter 4.)

Dyslexia assessment is undertaken by three groups of professionals:

1 **Chartered psychologists**. A psychologist's assessment consists of comprehensive tests of cognitive abilities (memory, perception, etc.) and literacy skills, and an analysis of how deficits that come to light in these areas will affect performance in the workplace. It is important to note that, while all Chartered Psychologists can offer general cognitive testing, only a minority specialize in assessing adult developmental dyslexia (specific learning difficulties). For further information on this, see Chapter 5.
2 **Dyslexia tutors.** Tutors work mainly in educational settings, and a tutor's assessment usually places emphasis on a detailed analysis of literacy and study skills, though some tests of general cognitive abilities may also be done.
3 **Job centre personnel**. Job centres usually offer dyslexia screening programmes, which may consist of, for example, interview, completion of a questionnaire and some simple tests of literacy skills.

In this chapter, we discuss general considerations concerning assessment and describe in detail a comprehensive psychological assessment; in Chapter 4, we review tests used by all three of the groups listed above; and in Chapter 5, we give a quick guide to arranging and appraising assessments.

Dyslexia has been described as essentially a cognitive deficit (Frith, 1995). As we saw in the previous chapter, the four areas in which deficits are most usually found are: phonological processing, short-term memory, sequencing and visuo-motor skills. We also saw that these underlying weaknesses are associated with an almost bewildering variety of difficulties, ranging from poor spelling and slow handwriting to problems with map reading, keeping a filing system, and getting to an appointment on time. One aim of a dyslexia assessment, therefore, should be to identify underlying deficits and to trace their consequences in every aspect of the client's life. This includes an appraisal not only of literacy, study, work, organizational and life skills, but also of the effect the difficulties have had on the client's educational and work history, and the way they have affected him emotionally.

A second aim of the assessment is to gain an idea of the client's general intellectual level, and hence his academic/professional potential. This is obviously important in counselling the client on possible career or study options and in recommending appropriate help: a person with specific learning difficulties has different needs from someone with a general learning difficulty.

A third aim of the assessment is to identify discrepancies between potential and achievement, and between various aspects of cognitive functioning or literacy skills.

Until recently, dyslexia was usually *defined* as a discrepancy between potential and attainment. A dyslexic person was deemed to be someone of average or above-average intelligence whose literacy skills were not commensurate with his intellectual abilities. More recently, however, many researchers have inclined to the view that dyslexia is more usefully characterized as a core weakness in phonological processing skills. If this is the case, then obviously people of below-average intelligence are just as entitled to be dyslexic as those of above-average intellectual ability. Nonetheless, it remains the case that obvious discrepancies between intellectual potential and literacy attainments, even if these cannot be taken as a definition of dyslexia, are still one of the strongest *indications* that dyslexic difficulties may be present.

In dyslexic children, such a discrepancy is usually plain to see on the basis of standardized reading and spelling tests; in the assessment of adults, however, more searching measures of literacy skills (and particularly speed of working) need to be used.

As well as looking for a discrepancy between attainment and potential, the assessor will be on the alert for other types of discrepancies that may indicate dyslexic difficulties. Turner (1997), who sums up this approach as a search for an 'unexpected failing', lists the following candidates:

- verbal vs. non-verbal ability
- non-verbal vs. spatial ability

- perceptual vs. motor ability
- reading vs. spelling
- decoding vs. comprehension
- literacy vs. numeracy
- word reading vs non-word reading.

Other discrepancies mentioned in the research literature are those between oral and writing abilities, and between listening and reading comprehension.

As noted above, many researchers consider the principal 'failing' in dyslexia to be a deficit in phonological processing skills. However, work on this hypothesis has not yet progressed to the stage where standardized tests have been produced for adults; nor indeed do all researchers agree that poor phonological processing should be regarded as the core deficit in dyslexia. Not all dyslexics have been found to have such deficits, and in some cases it seems that the difficulties are more in the area of perceptual processing and motor co-ordination.

Rack (personal communication) has suggested that it might be useful to distinguish four main areas of dyslexic difficulty:

- poor phonological ability
- poor visuo-spatial ability
- general slowness in reading and writing
- 'executive' difficulties, i.e. difficulties with tasks in which sequencing and structuring are involved (for example, composing an essay, keeping track of work commitments).

From this it is clear that assessing dyslexic difficulties is not an exact science: the assessor is usually not applying one single criterion in 'pronouncing' a client dyslexic, but taking into account a whole range of 'signs and symptoms', building up a broad picture from information gained from a variety of sources. Turner (1997) describes this as a *pointilliste* approach. Ideally, therefore, an assessment should include:

1 the taking of a detailed educational and occupational history
2 comprehensive assessment of cognitive abilities
3 assessment and detailed analysis of literacy and phonological processing skills
4 analysis of the way in which the results of (2) and (3) relate to the client's difficulties in his current job and/or course of study
5 consideration of emotional problems related to the dyslexic difficulties

6   referral to appropriate tutors, trainers or therapists, and provision of information regarding organizations that give help and advice to dyslexic employees and their employers.

These six components of a psychological assessment will now be looked at in more detail.

Educational and occupational history

Since there are only a limited number of formal tests that can be usefully administered to adults, it is particularly important to take into account previous educational and work history. A typical history is a late start with acquiring literacy skills at school and difficulty in passing formal examinations, such as GCSEs. Very often, the client will have achieved at least some modest academic or professional success later in life through his own efforts. He will quite probably find himself in a position which he feels does not recognize or utilize his true abilities, but will be hindered by constant inefficiency and carelessness from achieving promotion. Or, indeed, he may be unemployed, being prevented by a combination of poor literacy skills and lack of confidence from obtaining a job.

Cognitive abilities

For assessment of cognitive abilities, the test of choice is the WAIS, preferably the latest version, the WAIS-III UK. This provides a reliable measure of intellectual ability (general cognitive functioning) and a comprehensive cognitive profile. Statistically robust comparisons can be made between four ability areas: verbal, perceptual, working memory and speed of information processing. Dyslexics are frequently found to have good verbal (and general reasoning) ability, but poor memory and information processing skills. Dyspraxics often have a similar profile, but are also weak in perceptual and motor skills.

Close attention to the way the client performs on the WAIS tests gives many useful clues, too, to his general mode of working. It is useful to know, for instance, whether he responds in an impulsive and anxious manner, whether he is prepared to persevere with tasks he finds difficult, how far he uses verbal strategies for visual tasks, whether he tends to work in a random or systematic way, and, in cases where he fails on a task, whether this is through slowness or inaccuracy, or both.

The WAIS covers virtually all areas of cognitive functioning relevant to the assessment of dyslexic/dyspraxic difficulties; it may, however, be usefully supplemented by further tests of memory or perception, in particular of visual memory.

A particular advantage of an IQ assessment is that it points up not only weaknesses but strengths, thereby allowing the client to get a balanced view of his capabilities. Ott (1997) notes in particular that 'it can help to banish the misconception of being 'stupid' or 'thick' and can restore the battered ego of the dyslexic person, giving them a sense of purpose'.

Literacy and phonological processing skills

As regards literacy skills, the psychologist will be interested in the client's general level of competence in such areas as speed and accuracy of reading, reading comprehension, spelling, copying, note taking and free writing. Again, however, she will pay particular attention to qualitative aspects of the client's performance: the type of errors he makes, the way he approaches reading and writing tasks, whether he works in a fast and careless way, or whether he is slow but accurate.

A person with poor visual memory may tend to spell phonetically – thus he will spell regular words correctly but will 'regularize' the spelling of irregular words (colonel–cernul) and confuse homophones (straight–strait). A person with poor phonological skills, however, will have difficulty in spelling by ear: he will omit or wrongly position letters (refreshment–rerfeshmet).

It is important to give the client some *extended* passages of reading comprehension and writing, partly because many adult dyslexics achieve ceiling level on tests of single-word reading and spelling, and partly because it is a characteristic of dyslexics that they tire much more quickly than non-dyslexics when dealing with written material. Thus they often become increasingly inaccurate the longer they are required to read or write.

With writing, in particular, it is useful to ask the client to attempt at least two tasks: (i) to summarize a passage in a given period of time, and (ii) to write an extended piece about his job or course of study. These exercises give useful information about the client's ability to take notes, to plan and structure a written text and to write to a time limit, as well as indicating problems with syntax, punctuation and handwriting. They also allow an evaluation of fluency, style and use of vocabulary, and indicate whether there is a significant deterioration in spelling when the client has to write extended text.

Phonological processing skills can be tested in a number of ways. Particularly useful is a non-word reading test. Faced by a nonsense word, such as *kalputombromthrip*, the client cannot match this letter string with any word already in his internal dictionary, read it by analogy with another similar word or read it with the help of context; his only resource is to use phonology. Such a task, therefore, 'flushes out' poor phonological skills, and many a client who has sailed effortlessly through a single-word reading test founders on non-word reading. Other tasks that might be used to examine phonological processing skills include digit naming, verbal fluency, spoonerisms, and repeating polysyllabic words and non-words.

On all the reading tests described above, it is preferable if speed measures as well as accuracy measures are used. Adult dyslexics, especially 'well-compensated' ones, can often read accurately if given sufficient time, and so will perform well, often at ceiling level, on most reading tests. However, their speed of reading (especially when reading for comprehension) tends to be slower than that of non-dyslexics. There are virtually no standardized reading tests with speed norms for adults, but psychologists may collect their own informal norms, or use relevant data from research studies.

Practical implications

While the pattern of difficulty in cognitive and literacy tasks may be broadly similar for most dyslexics, the practical difficulties the dyslexic faces at work are obviously related to the particular nature of each person's job. It is therefore important to discuss in detail with each client the nature of their work, the particular demands it makes upon them and the special difficulties it presents.

With writing skills, for example, the first step is to ascertain from the client the precise types of writing tasks he is required to perform in his job. Is he required to write letters? Memos? Reports? Does he have to take notes at meetings or copy written material?

If the client works with numbers, then there needs to be an analysis of his accuracy and efficiency in basic figure work, such as data entry, copying and presentation.

With reading, again it is important to learn the precise nature of the material that the employee is required to read: Technical manuals? Government reports? Minutes of meetings? Is he required to take notes from and summarize written text?

What are the effects on the client's work of poor memory and organizational skills? Is the client in a job where he has to take telephone messages, follow written or spoken instructions, or keep to strict deadlines?

Communication skills, too, need to be considered. Is the client expected to undertake oral presentation of papers or reports at meetings? Does he have to explain things to clients or trainees? Does he have to deal at short notice with queries from the general public?

It is very important to be alert for signs of dyspraxic difficulties, as these are often missed. The client might report, for instance, that he is generally clumsy in manual tasks, or that he has difficulty in, for example, following left–right instructions, sorting letters in date order, filing or map reading.

In general, there needs to be a detailed analysis of the tasks the client has to undertake in his working day, and a consideration of the overall organization of the client's work schedule. It is often useful, if permission is given, to liaise with the client's manager to obtain some idea of how the client's difficulties are seen – and dealt with – by those around him.

Emotional factors

During the assessment session, the client's emotional reactions to his difficulties can be fully discussed. In some cases, employees have become so sensitive about their difficulties, and so worried about the implications of these for their future employment, that they have developed physical symptoms – insomnia, morning sickness, panic attacks on their journey to work or in the office. Or they may live in a state of chronic anxiety or depression.

In adults, the cluster of emotions surrounding dyslexic difficulties can be as much a problem as the difficulties themselves, and further consideration is given to this topic in Chapters 7 and 16.

In some cases, it may be necessary to discuss with a client the possibility of his making a radical decision about a career change. Although this may initially seem threatening, it may well eventually prove to be a sound move. For example, a dyslexic person who is performing with gross inefficiency as a clerk in an accounts department may feel encouraged to look for a job that requires less precision with numbers but more initiative or creativity. In most cases, however, the client simply needs help to become more efficient in the job that he holds, or to develop the skills he needs to apply for a promotion.

Help

There are a number of avenues of help a psychologist may suggest. If particular difficulties have come to light on the IQ test battery, the psychologist may refer the client on to another specialist: to a language or speech therapist if writing or oral skills are poor, to an orthoptist if there are visual problems, to a perceptual therapist, physiotherapist or occupational therapist if there are deficiencies in visuo-motor skills. She will also be able to refer the client to a specialist dyslexia tutor or trainer for help with all aspects of literacy and workplace skills.

If emotional problems are judged to be a straightforward consequence of dyslexic difficulties, then it may be appropriate to refer the client to a behaviour therapist who can teach specific programmes for managing stress and anxiety. In some cases, the distress surrounding the dyslexic difficulties is tangled with more deep-seated worries. For example, a person whose general upbringing has made him prone to feelings of worthlessness or lack of self-esteem will often regard his dyslexic problems as yet more proof that he has no value – and may consequently get these problems quite out of proportion. In such a case, a referral to a counsellor or psychotherapist may be appropriate.

Finally, the psychologist can offer to liaise with the client's manager or employer to discuss ways in which office procedures and the office environment can be adapted to accommodate the dyslexic person's difficulties and enable him to utilize his strengths. (Further guidance for employers is given in Chapter 18).

Summary

A psychological assessment of dyslexia should take account of – and show the links between – a client's educational and occupational history, his cognitive functioning and literacy skills, his current difficulties and his emotional state. Specific recommendations for tuition or training should be given and appropriate referrals made, if necessary, to other specialists. All this information should be provided in a detailed written report given to the client.

Many people initially approach a psychological assessment with apprehension, and it goes without saying that the onus is on the psychologist to endeavour to put the client at ease, to explain the purpose of the various tests administered (some of which might otherwise seem childish) and to give clear feedback about the results during or at the end of the session. In these circumstances, an assessment will generally turn out to be both enlightening and reassuring: it gives the client a useful opportunity to take stock of his life and enables him to plan for the future on the basis of a sound understanding of both his difficulties and strengths.

Further reading:

Bartlett D, Moody S (2000). Assessing and Managing Developmental Dyslexia in the Workplace. Journal of the Application of Occupational Psychology to Employment and Disability. 2, 2, 27–35.

Kirk J, Reid G (2000) Report on best practice in assessment and support for dyslexic adults. Employment Service, Occupational Psychology Division (in press).

McLoughlin D, Fitzgibbon G, Young V (1994) Adult Dyslexia: assessment, counselling and training. London: Whurr.

Chapter 3
Judgement day: Tom goes for an assessment

The idea of being assessed is always a daunting one and dyslexic clients have reported – or evinced – a variety of emotions before, during and after their assessment. In the following passage, all these emotions have been brought together in one fictional character, Tom. Tom writes as follows.

So – it was finally upon me: the Day of the Assessment or, as it seemed to me, Judgement Day. I had put off making the appointment with the psychologist for weeks, but I couldn't put it off for ever. My wife was badgering me, the children were encouraging me, friends were lecturing me. They had all become convinced that I was dyslexic. They had heard programmes about it, read books about it, talked to people about it – and now they were absolutely *positive* I was dyslexic. But I didn't feel so sure.

True, all my life I'd struggled with reading and writing. True, I'd always felt in a muddle somehow – but surely that was just me. At school I'd been put down as 'lazy', 'not very bright'; at college I had to work twice as hard as everyone else just to survive; and at work I was constantly in trouble for forgetting things and making silly mistakes.

I always seemed to be battling somehow. Battling to express myself, battling to take in what people were saying, battling to organize myself, battling to keep some self-respect in the face of constant frustration and humiliation.

And now suddenly people were telling me, 'No, this isn't stupidity, it isn't laziness or bloody-mindedness, it isn't anything terrible at all – it's just a collection of difficulties that you can do something about.' I felt I didn't know what to believe about myself.

As I drove to the assessment, I began to fear the worst. I felt my hands clammy and my heart beating. What dreadful revelations would there be about me?

And indeed, as the assessment progressed, I felt that my worst fears were being realized. I found it hard to give the psychologist any sort of coherent account of my problems; and, even though the tests were quite straightforward, I could feel myself getting panicky and making a mess of simple things. The reading and writing bits were the worst; I could hear myself stumbling over words, and a little composition I tried to write came out like gibberish.

I felt despondent and defeated and waited miserably for the psychologist's 'pronouncement'. Somewhere far off, almost in another world, I heard her saying, 'Well, Mr Jones...' and then I just caught phrases: 'no problems with your reasoning power ... very great potential ... hampered throughout life by dyslexic difficulties ... done tremendously well in the circumstances ... just need some specialist tuition'.

I felt numb for a few moments – then an overwhelming sense of relief. To my amazement I found I'd burst into tears – as if 40 years of damned up frustration and worry about myself suddenly flooded out.

I felt embarrassed about being so emotional though at the same time it made me feel a lot better. In fact, as I left the psychologist's office, I found myself grinning in a silly sort of way. I was gripped by a kind of elation – I almost floated back to the car. I was all right! It seemed as though some massive distortion in my life had suddenly been straightened out. I wasn't a fool, I wasn't a sluggard, I wasn't a lost cause, I had some perfectly ordinary difficulties that I could get help for.

I bought some flowers and a bottle of wine and went home. The family were waiting for me all agog. They spent the evening saying 'told you so' in various ways, but I couldn't explain to them what a world of difference there is between people telling you something and you really knowing it yourself.

For a day or so my feelings of elation continued, but, as the days passed and I started to take in the implications of what had happened, my mood changed. I began to have feelings of resentment, anger, rage that I had spent so many years thinking so little of myself, so many years hiding from the world, concealing some dark secret that was a mystery even to me. Bitterly I remembered the moments of humiliation, the periods of despair.

It almost seemed as if I'd spent 40 years in the wrong life. Forty years being confused about myself and bewildered by my behaviour. Forty years squandering energy in erecting defences against myself. How much more could I have done in life had I been free of all that fear and bewilderment?

To the dismay of my family and friends, I began to sink into despondency, even depression. I just felt that half my life had been lost and there was no way of getting it back. I suppose there was only one word for what I was feeling: grief. Grief for the loss of what might have been. Like all grief it was a very painful experience.

But I knew that I had to confront it and accept the losses of the past if I was to turn my life around in the future. So I did confront it – I sat it out, and at least the family were sensible enough not to try to jolly me out of it.

Eventually I surfaced again – with a strong resolve to give myself a future that was better than the past. I signed on with a tutor and began to talk through my difficulties and to learn ways of dealing with them. I was still prone to periods of anger and depression, but these gradually grew less.

I think one of the most positive things to come out of this is that the energy I used to put into 'hiding' now goes into finding constructive ways of dealing with my problems. I've got more confident too – I appreciate my good points and don't see myself simply as a liability to people as I did in the past.

And I am not afraid to ask for help either: I asked a friend to help me write this piece – but I can assure you that the emotions described here are very much my own!

Chapter 4
Assessment: tests

In this chapter we describe tests of cognitive (intellectual) ability and literacy skills that are commonly used in dyslexia assessments.

Tests of cognitive ability

The standard test of adult cognitive abilities is the Wechsler Adult Intelligence Scale (currently available in two versions, the WAIS-R and the more recent – and much superior – WAIS-III UK). This is the most widely used test of adult intelligence in the world, and is regarded as being both valid and reliable. It provides a cognitive profile that can be checked for dyslexic characteristics and has statistical properties that allow the user to detect specific weaknesses beyond natural variation.

There is no generally agreed definition of intelligence, but it can be said that the WAIS gives a useful picture of general cognitive functioning. It comprises two scales: a Verbal scale, which tests spoken language ability, and a Performance scale, which tests visual perception and visuo-motor skills. If the Verbal and Performance scores that emerge are fairly similar then a calculation can be performed that produces an overall IQ score. However, if the Verbal and Performance scores are dissimilar, then they are quoted separately. In the WAIS-III UK version of the test, the scale also yields four index scores, which give a more precise measure of verbal comprehension, perceptual organization, working memory and processing speed.

The subtests on the WAIS are as follows.

Verbal scale

Information: a test of general knowledge, and information retrieval from long-term memory.

Digit Span (repeating strings of numbers): a test of auditory short-term memory, sequencing ability and attention control.

Vocabulary: a test of vocabulary level, word comprehension and verbal fluency.

Arithmetic: a test of mental arithmetic, which is presented orally and which therefore taps auditory short-term memory; it gives some indication of the ability to concentrate and to follow oral directions accurately.

Comprehension: a test of practical judgement and common sense understanding of social rules, as well as verbal fluency.

Similarities: a test of verbal reasoning and abstract thinking ability, and also the ability to distinguish between the essential and the superficial; it is regarded as the best indicator of verbal ability and academic potential.

*Letter–Number Sequencing: a test of short-term memory, similar to digit span, but containing both numbers and letters.

Performance scale

Picture Completion (spotting missing details in pictures): a test of visual perception, alertness and memory.

Picture Arrangement (sequencing pictures to tell a story): a test of logical thinking, sequencing and comprehension of a total social situation.

Block Design (reproduction of designs with coloured blocks): tests spatial, perceptual and manipulative skills using abstract material.

Object Assembly (assembling small jigsaws): tests spatial, perceptual and manipulative skills with pictorial material, and in particular the ability to perceive a 'gestalt' and part–whole relationships.

Digit Symbol-Coding: a timed copying test, which requires good hand–eye co-ordination and which taps visual short-term memory, visual orientation and tracking skill.

*Matrix Reasoning: a test of non-verbal reasoning in a multiple choice format; the client has to choose a design which completes a pattern.

*Symbol Search: a test of speed of information processing with visually presented material.

(*The tests marked with an asterisk are recent additions to the scale, included only in the most recent version of the WAIS, i.e. the WAIS-III UK.)

The pattern of scores on these subtests provides a cognitive 'map' of the person being tested, pointing up both strengths and weaknesses.

Certain patterns of scores are frequently associated with dyslexic and/or dyspraxic difficulties, though it must be stressed that a particular type of cognitive profile alone is not sufficient evidence for a diagnosis. Some individuals may have compensated for their cognitive weaknesses well enough to acquire good literacy skills. However, if *no* significant cognitive weaknesses are found, then caution needs to be exercised in making a diagnosis of dyslexia.

Strong evidence in support of a dyslexia diagnosis would be a significant difference between scores on the Verbal Comprehension index and scores on the Working Memory and/or Processing Speed index. If there were also significant differences between the Verbal Comprehension index and the Perceptual Organization index, then dyspraxic difficulties may also be indicated.

In assessing whether a difference between scores is significant, it is necessary to determine two things: (i) if the difference is statistically significant, i.e. that it is not the result of measurement error; and (ii) that it is clinically significant, i.e. that the difference occurs only rarely in the general population.

Shown below are two cognitive profiles, one of an adult who has predominantly dyslexic difficulties, and one of an adult who has predominantly dyspraxic difficulties. (In practice, mixed profiles may also be found.)

Cognitive profile suggesting dyslexic difficulties

IQ and index scores
Average range: 90–110

Full-scale IQ =	103	Verbal Comprehension:	114
Verbal IQ =	96	Perceptual Organization:	123
Performance IQ =	111	Working Memory:	78
		Processing Speed:	93

Index sub-tests
Range: 1–19. Average range: 9–11

Verbal Comprehension (VC)		**Perceptual Organization (PO)**	
Vocabulary	11	Picture Completion	15
Similarities	15	Block Design	16
Information	12	Matrix Reasoning	10

Working Memory (WM)

Digit Span	8
Arithmetic	5
Letter–Number Sequencing	6

Processing Speed (PS)

Digit Symbol-Coding	8
Symbol Search	10

Other tests

Comprehension	17

Picture Arrangement	11
Object Assembly	15

Statistically significant differences were found between the following index scores (frequency of magnitude of difference in the general population given in brackets):

VC	WM	(1%)
VC	PS	(17%)

In the above profile it can be seen that the client performs much better on verbal tasks than on tasks which tap working memory and processing speed. His weakness in memory is particularly severe being at a level found in only 1% of the population.

Within the subset of verbal tests, the client does less well on Vocabulary and Information than on the reasoning test (Similarities). Within the performance subset he has relatively poor scores on Picture Arrangement, a sequencing task, and Matrix Reasoning. These relative weaknesses are often seen in a dyslexic profile (for further discussion, see p. 32). A client with this cognitive profile may well turn out to be a classic phonological dyslexic.

Cognitive profile suggesting dyspraxic difficulties

IQ and index scores
Average range: 90–110

Full-scale IQ =	100	Verbal Comprehension:	114
Verbal IQ =	112	Perceptual Organization:	89
Performance IQ =	85	Working Memory:	108
		Processing Speed:	84

Index sub-tests
Range: 1–19.   Average range: 9–11

Verbal Comprehension (VC)

Vocabulary	12
Similarities	14
Information	12

Perceptual Organization (PO)

Picture Completion	12
Block Design	6
Matrix Reasoning	7

Working Memory (WM)

Digit Span	12
Arithmetic	11
Letter–Number Sequencing	11

Processing Speed (PS)

Digit Symbol-Coding	6
Symbol Search	8

Other tests

Comprehension	14

Picture Arrangement	10
Object Assembly	11

Statistically significant differences were found between the following index scores (frequency of magnitude of difference in the general population given in brackets):

VC PO   (3%)
VC PS   (5%)

In this case the client performed much better on verbal tests than on tests which tap perceptual skills and processing speed. Auditory short-term memory was relatively good. A client with such a cognitive profile might learn to read reasonably well, but might have difficulty with spelling, writing, maths and organizational skills.

It may be noted that, if a client has both dyslexic and dyspraxic difficulties, then the overall Verbal and Performance IQ scores may not be very different; in such a case, comparisons between index scores (and between individual subtest scores) would be crucial.

It can be seen from the above that the WAIS is a comprehensive and informative cognitive test: if it does have an Achilles heel it is the lack of a strong test of visual short-term memory. Consequently it may usefully be supplemented by a visual memory test from another battery, e.g. the British Ability Scales (BAS) or the Wechsler Memory Scale (WMS-III UK). The latter includes tests of immediate, delayed and working memory (both auditory and visual) and is co-normed with the WAIS.

All the above tests are 'closed' tests, that is, they are available only to psychologists who have had relevant training in psychometric testing. The cognitive tests available to non-psychologist assessors are less satisfactory. The most frequently used are probably the Mill Hill Vocabulary Scale (Ravens Vocabulary Scales) and matrices tests, such as the Ravens Progressive Matrices. However, there are concerns about the validity of these tests: the norms have been criticized (Turner 1997), and in the case of the Mill Hill, it is considered that too few vocabulary items cover each vocabulary range (National Working Party Report on Dyslexia in Higher Education, 1999).

Another choice for a test of general abilities would be the Kaufman Brief Intelligence Test. This consists of one non-verbal reasoning test (Matrices) and two verbal tests (Expressive Vocabulary and Definitions); the latter two are combined into a single vocabulary score. A drawback is that the Definitions test contains a reading component (and uses American spelling), but it is possible to use the Expressive Vocabulary test only, and to predict a Definitions score from this.

A further consideration is that tests such as vocabulary scales and matrices have limited usefulness in the context of a dyslexia assessment. The scores they yield do not form part of a comprehensive cognitive profile, and consequently they could be misleading. In particular, they might produce *an underestimate of intellectual ability* – something that dyslexic people have long been trying to escape. It has already been noted that, on the WAIS profile of dyslexic/dyspraxic people, the Vocabulary score is often relatively low, and evidence from the research literature, too, suggests that vocabulary acquisition is impeded in dyslexia. Consequently an estimate of intellectual ability based on a vocabulary test could be an underestimate.

Matrices tests could be similarly misleading: a high score on such a test might be regarded as indicative of high intellectual ability, but an average to low score would be hard to interpret. Although matrices tests are designed to give a measure of reasoning ability rather than visuo-spatial skills, performance on these tests does depend on, among other things, attention to visual detail, distinguishing between left and right and the ability to mentally rotate abstract forms. In consequence, people who have significant dyspraxic difficulties might do badly on these tests, not because of poor reasoning ability, but because of weak visuo-spatial skills.

It has also been noted (Turner, 1997) that matrices tests can cause difficulty to dyslexics (who are not dyspraxic). This may be because these tests are complex tasks that tap verbal as well as non-verbal abilities, and which require the ability to manage a large set of problem-solving goals in working memory (Carpenter et al., 1990).

The WAIS-III UK Technical Manual reports moderately positive correlations of between 0.5 and 0.7 between the Ravens PM and the predecessors of the WAIS-III. However, a study on a group of *dyslexic* students at Sheffield University produced a positive correlation of only 0.3 between the two tests (Fawcett, personal communication). In general, therefore, estimates of cognitive abilities based on matrices tests need to be treated with caution in the context of a dyslexia assessment.

Reading and spelling

Tests of reading should include both tests of single-word reading and of reading comprehension. As noted in the previous chapter, it is important that measures of both accuracy and speed are taken, since many adult dyslexics, especially those who have compensated well for their difficulties, achieve good scores on reading tests on which there is no time limit. However, their difficulties may be evident in the slowness of their reading. There are few standardized tests with time norms; however, enterprising assessors could use norms from research data or collect their own informal norms. (It is better to record the time a client takes to complete a test rather than to put a time limit on the test.)

Tests of single-word reading appropriate for adults are the Wide Range Achievement Test (WRAT-3), which is a screening test, and the Woodcock Reading Mastery Tests. Both have an age range of 5–75 years, though both suffer from the disadvantage that they have US norms. Normed on a British population, and shortly to be co-normed with the WAIS-III UK, is the National Adult Reading Test.

A timed oral test of text reading is a good discriminator between dyslexics and non-dyslexics, the former often reading around 30–50 percent more slowly than the latter. (The passage used needs to be just within the reading competence of the client.)

It is not at present easy to find an entirely satisfactory test for reading comprehension. The NFER Reading Comprehension Test (EH 2), however, can make a useful contribution. (This test is no longer published but copies of it are still in circulation.) It consists of seven passages of text and multiple choice questions. Its age range is only 11:0 to 15:11 years and its accuracy norms are somewhat dated, but it can usefully be administered as a timed test: a dyslexic adult often takes twice or even three times as long as a non-dyslexic person to complete it. Also useful is the Scholastic Abilities Test for Adults (SATA), which has written questions and multiple choice answers.

A test often used in a workplace context is the Spadafore Diagnostic Reading Test. This is a test of single-word reading, prose reading, reading comprehension and listening comprehension. It has an age range from school age to adult, and measures reading ability in terms of professional, technical, vocational and functional levels. The fact that this test is criterion-referenced and uses US spellings may limit its usefulness.

A test of passage comprehension is also included in the Woodcock Reading Mastery Tests, mentioned above.

For spelling, appropriate tests can be found in the WRAT-3, mentioned above, and also in Level 5 of the British Spelling Tests (BST). The latter has the advantage of having UK norms, but is very lengthy to administer (it takes approximately 30 minutes).

As well as using a formal spelling test, it is useful to look at the way the client spells particular types of words, for example, regular polysyllabic words, irregular words, homophones and words that require knowledge of spelling rules. This both gives insight into underlying difficulties and provides a baseline for tuition.

Writing

There are virtually no normed tests for writing, but a number of tasks may be set which will give the assessor an idea of such things as: speed, neatness, accuracy, style, fluency, grammar, punctuation, use of vocabulary, and the ability to plan and structure written work and write to a time limit. It is also important to note if spelling deteriorates markedly when the client is writing a lengthy piece, and whether he is able to spot his mistakes when asked to proof-read his work.

Tasks that might be given include: a dictation exercise, making a summary of a passage (presented orally and/or in writing) and free writing. It may also be useful to get an idea of the way the client approaches particular writing tasks that are a requirement of his job, e.g. copying figures or writing letters.

Phonological processing skills

Since adult dyslexics may have become reasonably adept at reading and spelling words, it is important to administer tests that tap their underlying phonological abilities.

Non-word reading, a task that requires both phonological ability and phonic knowledge, is regarded as an excellent marker for dyslexia (Rack et al., 1992). Generally, dyslexics are more inaccurate than normal readers in reading non-words (especially those of three or more syllables), and they are almost always slower on this task. The client may, therefore, be asked to read a series of non-words of increasing length, and possibly also extended passages which contain some nonsense words. An example of such a passage would be:

The wizpak took a zasty potlich and weddled it into the cramdittle. 'Hulapadoo!' he cried, 'now we can wortle a pampoliast and the nakrons will be decabulous'.

There are few standardized tests of non-word reading for adults, but, again, assessors can collect informal norms or use norms from research papers (e.g. Gross Glenn et al., 1990; Gallagher et al., 1996).

Other tests of phonological abilities currently to be found in research studies are: repetition of polysyllabic words and non-words, rhyming tasks, syllable deletion, syllable counting, odd-one-out tasks, picture naming, speeded naming (for pictures and digits), verbal fluency and spoonerisms (see Chapter 19 for more details).

Arithmetic

An arithmetic test (age range 5–75 years) is included in the WRAT-3, mentioned above. In general, however, it is less important to test adults formally on arithmetic than to check if they can cope with the practical number tasks that are involved in their work, e.g. writing down figures correctly, giving correct change, using a calculator accurately.

Screening tests

Screening is usually done by a combination of interview and questionnaire, though a standardized assessment of literacy skills, such as the WRAT-3, may be used. A frequently used test is the Bangor Dyslexia Test, though this has an age range of only 7–18 years and is not very discriminating when used with adults; however it does give some insight into difficulties in a range of non-literacy skills often associated with dyslexia.

A screening test devised specifically for adults is the Dyslexia Adult Screening Test (DAST). This consists of 11 subtests, including reading, spelling and cognitive tasks that are generally believed to be sensitive to dyslexia. A particular advantage of this test is that it includes some timed tests, e.g. of naming, reading and spelling.

There are also two standardized self-administered computer programs, the Dyslexia Test and Quick Scan, but these have only recently come on to the market and details of predictive validity and reliability have not yet been published.

Questionnaires (available from the main dyslexia organizations) also give some indication of whether dyslexic/dyspraxic difficulties might be present. Examples of such questionnaires are given in Appendix A.

These then are some of the tests that may be used in a dyslexia assessment. In general, an assessment should strike a balance between assessing general intellectual abilities on the one hand, and literacy/numeracy skills on the other. It can be expected to take about three hours, with approximately two hours of this being taken up with tests, leaving around an hour for history taking, feedback on the tests, and general discussion and counselling.

Since it is not easy for a dyslexic/dyspraxic person to know whether any assessment that is offered to him is adequate to his needs, brief guidance on this is given in the following chapter.

Further reading

Beech JR, Singleton CH (eds) (1997) The Psychological Assessment of Reading. London: Routledge.
Turner M (1997) Psychological Assessment of Dyslexia. London:Whurr.

Test publishers

('R' denotes tests restricted to use by qualified psychologists)
Bangor Dyslexia Test (1997): LDA, Wisbech, Cambridgeshire.
British Ability Scales (BAS-II) (1996): NFER-Nelson. (R)
British Spelling tests (BST) (1998): NFER-Nelson.
Dyslexia Adult Screening Test (DAST) (1999): The Psychological Corporation.
Kaufman Brief Intelligence Test (K-BIT) (1990): American Guidance Services, Circle Pines, Minnesota, USA. UK supplier: Dyslexia Institute.
Mill Hill Vocabulary Scale (Ravens Vocabulary Scales) (1994): Oxford Psychologists Press.
National Adult Reading Test (1982): NFER-Nelson.
Ravens Progressive Matrices (Advanced) (1947): Oxford Psychologists Press.
Scholastic Abilities Test for Adults (SATA) (1991): Pro-Ed, Austin, Texas, USA.
Spadafore Diagnostic Reading Test (1983): Academic Therapy Publications, USA. UK supplier: Ann Arbor.
Wechsler Adult Intelligence Scale (WAIS-III UK) (1999): Psychological Corporation. (R)

Wechsler Memory Scale (WMS-III UK): (1999): The Psychological Corporation. (R)
Wide Range Achievement Test (WRAT-3) (1993): The Psychological Corporation.
Woodcock Reading Mastery Tests (1987): American Guidance Services, Circle Pines,
    Minnesota, USA. UK supplier: Dyslexia Institute.

Chapter 5
Assessing the assessors: a rough guide for punters

In this chapter we present brief guidelines on how to find an assessor and what to look for in an assessment.

How to find a suitably qualified psychologist

Adults who have dyslexic difficulties are often advised to seek an assessment from a Chartered Psychologist. There are five main groups of Chartered Psychologists who may be able to offer such an assessment:

- educational psychologists
- clinical psychologists
- occupational psychologists
- neuropsychologists
- research psychologists.

However, only a small proportion of psychologists in each of these groups specializes in testing adults with developmental dyslexic (specific learning) difficulties. Psychologists whose practice is mainly with children or with people who have acquired dyslexia (due, for example, to stroke or head injury) may not use a sufficiently specialized test battery.

When you are arranging an assessment with a psychologist, do not hesitate to ask about his/her qualifications and experience. If you find it difficult to 'interrogate' the psychologist about this over the telephone, or if you are not clear about his/her response to your questions, then you could ask a representative of one of the dyslexia support organizations to 'assist you in your enquiries'. (See Chapter 21 for list.)

What the assessment should include

Dyslexic difficulties in adulthood are often subtle, and are not easily picked up by simple tests of reading and spelling. The assessment should, therefore, include both searching tests of literacy skills and also tests of general cognitive abilities, the latter being an important part of the adult dyslexic profile.

Tests of general cognitive abilities

The WAIS is the standard IQ test. It provides an IQ score and a comprehensive profile of cognitive abilities, including verbal reasoning, vocabulary, memory, perception, motor skills and speed of information processing. It may be supplemented by further tests of memory and perception (e.g. from the WMS or the BAS).

Tests of literacy skills

These should include tests of:

- single-word reading and spelling
- reading (and spelling) non-words
- timed oral reading
- a taxing and lengthy reading comprehension test using material appropriate for adults
- a lengthy piece of writing, allowing for an appraisal of: grammar, punctuation, handwriting, fluency and clarity of expression, ability to structure a written piece

Other tests which may be given could include dictation, and tests of phonological processing, such as phoneme deletion or spoonerisms.

It is useful if reading tests with norms for time as well as accuracy can be used, as dyslexic adults are often distinguished from their non-dyslexic counterparts by a slow speed of reading rather than inaccuracy.

It should be emphasized that a literacy assessment which consists only of single-word reading and spelling tests (and perhaps a very simple, short comprehension passage) is not adequate for the assessment of adult developmental dyslexia.

Assessment reports

The assessment report (which is generally at least five pages long) should clearly explain the implications of the results of the WAIS test and relate these meaningfully both to literacy attainments and to difficulties experienced in the workplace. It should give a full analysis of performance in literacy tests, including both level of performance and types of errors made. It should also give an indication of your areas of strength and of your academic/professional potential. Finally, it should proffer advice on how to manage any difficulties that emerge, and where to find specialist help for them.

What is the difference between a psychologist's and a tutor's assessment?

As regards the testing of literacy skills, there is no significant difference between a psychologist's and a tutor's assessment. As regards cognitive testing, however, there is a difference in that the main cognitive tests (WAIS, WMS, BAS) are 'closed' tests, available only to suitably qualified psychologists. Tutors will usually do some tests (e.g. vocabulary, matrices) which give a general idea of cognitive abilities; an assessment which consisted of tests of literacy alone would have too narrow a focus. Tutor assessors can be found through all the main dyslexia organisations.

What about dyspraxia?

Dyspraxic difficulties are often subsumed under the 'dyslexia' label, but, in cases where they are severe, it is preferable that they be separated out from dyslexia so that they can be appropriately treated and managed. Dyspraxic difficulties are most usually picked up from the WAIS profile, so, if your assessment does not include the WAIS, check with the assessor that some relevant tests have been done.

IQ profiling

If you wish to supplement a tutor's assessment with a WAIS (IQ) profile, this can be arranged through a chartered psychologist, but, again, be sure to choose a psychologist who is knowledgeable about dyslexic/dyspraxic difficulties.

Chapter 6
Dyspraxia observed

In this chapter we look at a range of weaknesses in perceptual and motor functioning that may be associated with dyslexic difficulties and which may result in inefficiency in many domestic and workplace tasks.

It is not easy to live always in the shadow of another person, to feel that this other person gets all the attention while one's own existence is ignored. Yet, this could well be the way that many dyspraxic people feel, for, while dyslexia has become widely recognized, dyspraxia still remains a 'Cinderella' condition. One reason for this, no doubt, is that dyspraxic difficulties go so much hand in hand with dyslexic ones that they are often simply included in a description of dyslexia and left, as it were, to fend for themselves under the dyslexia label.

The word 'dyspraxia' comes from the Greek 'praxis', which means 'doing, acting, deed, practice'. 'Dys', again from the Greek, means 'difficulty', and thus dyspraxia means literally 'difficulty with doing or acting'. The definition offered by Portwood (1999) is 'motor difficulties caused by perceptual problems, especially visual-motor and kinesthetic motor difficulties'. Kirby (1999) points out that medical professionals define dyspraxia very specifically as 'motor planning difficulties and perceptual problems'. In the educational world, however, the term is used more 'vaguely' to cover general clumsiness and poor visuo-spatial skills. (Kirby suggests that a better term for educationalists to use would be 'developmental co-ordination disorder'). In this chapter, as elsewhere in this book, the 'loose' definition has been used.

Early indications of dyspraxic difficulties in children are:

* lateness in starting to walk
* not passing through the usual crawling stage
* clumsiness

- difficulty with tasks such as tying shoelaces, fastening buttons, catching balls, riding a bicycle and telling the time.

The underlying difficulties persist into adulthood. A severely affected adult dyspraxic may have difficulty with gross motor skills: for example, he might have a clumsy gait, lack awareness of his body position in space, show a tendency to fall, trip over and bump into things. He may find it difficult to drive a car, to achieve good balance and body control, to play sports, especially bat and ball games, to dance or carry out any activity which requires rhythm, to play musical instruments and to walk up and down hills.

More commonly found in association with dyslexic difficulties are weaknesses in fine motor skills, also known as hand–eye co-ordination. These result in difficulty with such things as typing, sewing, using locks and keys, doing art and craft work, and performing domestic chores and mechanical tasks (such as repairing cars). There may be difficulty, too, with dressing, applying make-up and doing hair, and co-ordination problems with eating and drinking.

In terms of literacy skills, handwriting is often seriously affected. There is also difficulty in keeping one's place on a page, being accurate with copying and proof-reading, and scanning columns of figures.

Associated perceptual difficulties cause problems with following instructions and protocols, discriminating between left and right and having a sense of time, direction, speed or weight. The combined weaknesses in perception and motor planning make driving a particularly hazardous occupation for dyspraxics. They find it difficult to judge distances as well as to manoeuvre the car successfully. Also, their poor sense of direction makes it difficult for them to follow maps and to find their way in strange, or even familiar, places.

With thinking and language, there may be difficulty in planning and organizing thoughts, remembering things and concentrating.

It has been noted that dyspraxia is sometimes associated with certain other disorders, such as attention deficit disorder (ADD) and hyperactivity. In adults, ADD is usually characterized by inattentiveness, disorganization and impulsivity. It is thought, too, that there can be a link with Asperger's syndrome.

As has been noted above, there is a wide overlap between dyslexic and dyspraxic difficulties. A dyspraxic person will almost certainly have some dyslexic difficulties, though the converse is not always true (since dyslexic difficulties may be due primarily to poor phonological skills).

The fact that dyspraxic difficulties are often overshadowed by dyslexic ones is very disadvantageous to dyspraxic people: their specific motor and perceptual difficulties often go unrecognized, as does the fact that the type of remedial programme needed by someone who is predominantly dyspraxic is different from that needed by someone who is predominantly dyslexic. A dyslexic may need to work chiefly on phonological, literacy and study skills, and will usually need to be seen by an educational/clinical psychologist and dyslexia/study skills tutor. The dyspraxic person, however, will need, in addition to the above, an assessment of motor/perceptual skills and remedial help from, for example, a physiotherapist, occupational therapist or perceptual therapist. (Such help may be available on the NHS.)

In the opening pages of this book, we followed a dyslexic employee through his day at the office. A dyspraxic person would encounter many similar difficulties, but also some that are more particularly in the dyspraxic sphere. Marianne, an adult with severe dyspraxic problems, gives the following list of things that can go wrong during her working day:

1 Arrive late at work because a diversion on the roads meant I couldn't follow my usual route. I looked at the map and worked out an alternative route. I started to drive again, but almost immediately I lost the image of the map. I arrived at a junction and had no idea which way to go. The signs didn't seem to help me. I panicked and got lost. It was a nightmare. Eventually a taxi driver helped me find my way.
2 Had to do some photocopying on the new complicated photocopier. I could not remember how to work it although I'd had some brief instruction the day before.
3 I had to enter some data on the computer, which I do much more slowly than everybody else partly because I type slowly and partly because I make many typing errors. I felt overwhelmed by the amount of work I had to do and made quite a few mistakes. Even after proof-reading what I had written I still missed many of the mistakes. I just couldn't seem to see them.
4 I had to copy down some figures and was unable to copy them correctly and in the proper columns.
5 I was asked to find a document on my desk which someone had given me just half an hour ago. I couldn't find it among the jumble of stuff there and wasted a lot of time looking for it in the wrong place. Later I found it where I first started to look for it but somehow I hadn't seen it the first time.
6 In the meantime my work was piling up and the telephone kept ringing. I wrote down something that somebody wanted on a scrap of paper. Later I found I couldn't read my writing.

7 Later in the day I had to stamp some of the documents with a date
   stamp. It still had the previous day's date on it. I tried to move the
   number with a pencil but it got stuck and then suddenly both the
   month and the day moved on and could not be separated easily. I had
   to give it to someone else to sort out.
8 Overall it's no wonder that nobody respects me or lets me do anything
   but the most basic stuff. I need help all the time and I keep making
   mistakes. The more I get told off about it the more mistakes I make
   and the more stressed I become. I can't work at the rate that other
   people do. I hate work.

Dyspraxic difficulties might feel overwhelming, but, like dyslexic difficulties, they can be alleviated and circumvented in various ways. Help can
be given with perceptual and motor skills, time management, concentration and organizational skills. Lynn, a dyspraxic woman, writes as
follows.

> About two years ago I came across an article in a newsletter that was to
> change my whole perception of myself. It was an account of the difficulties
> experienced by a woman with developmental dyspraxia and I identified
> with almost all of the problems she mentioned. I was literally reduced to
> tears because she could have been describing my life. And also the stark
> realization that I had reached the age of 39 before discovering what was
> wrong with me!
>
> My main problem was a lack of spatial awareness, inability to judge
> speed and distance, no sense of direction, inability to read maps and bouts
> of depression and agoraphobia. When younger I had terrible problems
> learning to tell the time, riding a bike, roller skating, also playing any sport,
> especially involving hand to eye skills, painful shyness and reluctance to
> join in any group activities, such as parties or team sports – the list is
> endless.
>
> However, since I have been encouraged to find out more about the
> condition, I've had an assessment and, after years of low esteem, I am now
> able to help myself understand and hopefully move forward from the
> negative attitudes of other people and also to inform them about dyspraxia
> and particular problems.

A final note on terminology: other terms for dyspraxia, or for various
components of it, are: development dyspraxia, developmental clumsiness, apraxia, minimal brain damage, perceptual-motor dysfunction,
sensory integrative dysfunction, motor-based learning difficulties, motor

neurological dysfunction and neuro-developmental delay. Clearly, the more ill-defined a condition, the more names it attracts. The important thing, however, is not so much which label is used, but whether a particular set of difficulties has been identified and appropriate help provided.

Further reading

Colley M (Ed) (2000) Living with Dyspraxia: a guide for adults with developmental dyspraxia. Dyspraxia Foundation Adult Support Group.

Portwood M (1999) Developmental Dyspraxia, A Practical Manual for Parents and Professionals. London: David Fulton.

Chapter 7
Emotional reactions

In this chapter we consider the wide range of emotions that dyslexic people may feel about their difficulties and their situation. Although in real life, of course, different emotions combine together, or conflict with one another, in this chapter they have been 'separated out'. In many cases, the descriptions are taken verbatim from the reports (written or spoken) of dyslexic clients. (In such cases, names have been changed to preserve confidentiality and the texts have been slightly edited).

Confusion and bewilderment

Nowadays dyslexic difficulties are often recognized while a child is still at school. Thus, whether or not appropriate help is available, the difficulties are at least acknowledged and information about them can be sought from appropriate organizations. Until recently, however, this was not the case. All too frequently dyslexic children were regarded as stupid or lazy or just plain puzzling. All those children who left school with unrecognized dyslexic difficulties are now adults, and their difficulties will not have gone away.

It is unfortunately the case that a large number, probably the majority, of these adult dyslexics are still unaware that they have a recognizable pattern of difficulties and that these difficulties can be significantly alleviated through the learning of appropriate skills and strategies. Typically, therefore, an adult dyslexic feels thoroughly confused about himself. He seems to be quite bright and quick-thinking in some ways, but apparently quite 'stupid' in others.

This feeling of being 'intelligently stupid' is well described by Annie, a 32-year-old woman who has recently realized that she is dyslexic. She left school without qualifications and now works as a filing clerk in a large company. She describes her view of her situation as follows:

Mainly I just feel I don't know who I am. Sometimes I feel quite good about myself. Sometimes when people tell me things I catch on quite quickly, quicker than other people, and then I feel I'm OK. Other times I don't understand what people are telling me and I make silly mistakes. I put files in the wrong place so that people can't find them.

I don't know how other people feel about me. When I'm talking to somebody at work, I ask myself: are they thinking 'stupid git' or are they thinking 'she's OK'?

I don't know who I am or what I'm capable of. I wish someone could tell me, I wish someone could sort me out.

Barry, a young engineering student, spoke more violently about similar feelings.

It's a mess – a f****** mess.

Embarrassment, shame and guilt

Charlie has been unemployed since he left school five years ago, but he occasionally picks up a job as a waiter in a café. He doesn't keep these jobs long, because a perennial problem for him is that he finds it difficult to remember and accurately write down the orders placed by the customers. In Charlie's words:

It's embarrassing. If there's three or four people at a table I don't take in what they say and have to ask a second time. Sometimes I'm still not sure I've got it, but I feel I can't keep on asking them. I just hope I've got it right. When the clients get the wrong food they complain, and make a fuss, and then there's a row. It always ends in the same way. The boss loses patience, and gives me the sack. I often feel I'd like to try and explain my difficulty to someone, but really it just feels too embarrassing, not to be able to do a simple thing – especially when I've got two A levels!

Feelings of embarrassment can deepen into shame, and, whereas embarrassment is often specific to a particular situation, shame seems to seep through the whole personality and colour the whole of a person's life.

Deirdre, now a wife and mother, worked briefly in the customer services department of a large company, but was very thankful to give up her job when she became pregnant with her first child. This is how Deirdre describes her feelings about herself:

It was a relief to stop working, really. I just felt I didn't want to face people. I was getting by at the office as long as I could follow my fixed routine and nothing new came up. Just as long as there was nothing urgent. When I did make mistakes I'd find ways to cover them up, and when things seemed too difficult I was quite good at getting colleagues to do things. I'd pretend I was too busy, or not feeling well, or find some excuse.

As time went on, the situation seemed to get worse. All I seemed to do all day was to tell lies, or avoid things, or cover things up, and on a couple of occasions I even put the blame on someone else for something I'd done wrong. When I look back on it now, I can see that that's what I did all day long – deceiving people. It was as if that was my job. I spent my time getting more and more efficient in deceiving.

Things at home were relatively okay. Dave, my husband, looked after our financial affairs and wrote any letters that needed to be sent to the Council or whatever. I didn't feel challenged at home in any way, I didn't have to practise deceit on Dave, but gradually I did start to feel I was deceiving him too. Not with another man, that would have been almost straightforward! I felt I was deceiving him by pretending to be somebody that I wasn't. I was pretending to be a working woman who was holding down a job and leading a normal office life. But I wasn't. I was this creature with a dreadful guilty secret. I felt I was just going through the motions, cooking, cleaning, even getting pregnant, and that it was all some sort of ridiculous sham. I wasn't worthy to be anyone's wife, I certainly wasn't worthy to be a mother.

In the end it was like I wasn't a person at all any longer. I was just a Guilty Secret, and I felt it was only a matter of time before somehow the whole thing would explode and I'd be exposed before the whole world as a fraud and a sham and a charlatan. It's easy to look back now and think I got it all out of proportion, which I did, but at the time that was my life. I just felt like a criminal. The feeling of shame was so terrible. It took away all pleasure in life, all pleasure in meeting people, for a time it even took away my pleasure in my family.

The feeling of having a guilty secret is something that is very commonly reported by dyslexic adults. Ella, a successful potter, describes it thus (speaking of herself in the third person):

But she, Ella, had a secret inside her. Well, she could not say it was exactly a secret. But she kept 'it' in a box; and would only open the lid very cautiously as there 'it' always was, in the box. She was getting better at lifting the lid, and taking the bits out, having a look, and even keeping some of them out on top of the box. You may well laugh when you know the contents of the box, and join all those people who never quite believe Ella.

It was dyslexia: that word, that almost indescribable thing, lived in the box and pervaded almost every part of her life, but no one could see it. It was a living nightmare.

Lack of confidence, low self-esteem

The emotions described above – bewilderment, shame, guilt – deal a crippling blow to confidence and self-esteem.

Lack of confidence manifests itself both in relation to specific tasks that a dyslexic person finds difficult, and in a more general way. A dyslexic person, whether or not his difficulties have been acknowledged and given a label, knows very well that he is inefficient in a number of aspects of his work. How hard it is to be assigned a task that you feel you will be unable to do.

This is an experience a dyslexic person will have had from childhood, perhaps even from being a toddler. While other children seem to progress almost carelessly through their developmental stages – walking, talking, tying shoelaces, telling the time, reading, writing – the dyslexic child finds himself in difficulty. He is slower to develop these abilities, and feels he is not performing them well. Very early on a sense of inadequacy, even impotence, sets in, a feeling that he won't be able to manage things, that he won't get them right. And this conviction does not go away.

Years later, in adult life, in everyday tasks, in workplace situations, the feeling still remains that he is lacking in the requisite abilities. When a simple task is performed –writing down a telephone number or writing a letter – a nagging feeling remains. Did I get that right?

In working life, this lack of confidence about the ability to perform specific tasks extends to a more general feeling of not being competent to hold down one's job. Then there is the question of applying for promotion, or applying for another job. In interviews, one needs to appear confident, but how can one be confident about how one would cope with a new challenge?

The daily questionings of one's own abilities and capacities will slowly but surely erode one's self-esteem. Among all the problems, the difficulties, the inefficiencies, the traumas, where is the person who is of worth? Is there such a person in there somewhere?

Faced with such nagging questions, people tend to react in one of two ways: either they become withdrawn and defensive, or they become truculent and aggressive. Both reactions are distortions of natural coping strategies. Neither of them makes life in the workplace any easier.

The defensive person can easily become reclusive – an outsider, who shrinks from contact with his colleagues and seems permanently preoccupied. He is often perceived to be sensitive, and people become afraid of upsetting him. Reservations about his work may not be openly expressed, and resentment against him may build up until one day there may be an explosion of anger against him.

The person who tries to hide lack of confidence behind an aggressive exterior becomes equally isolated. People feel apprehensive of approaching him, yet he is an easy target for anger and can quickly become the office scapegoat.

When a lack of confidence results in the aggressive or the defensive mode of behaviour, the dyslexic person concerned is trapped in a pattern of interaction, or rather reaction, which imprisons him in his own lonely and distressing world.

Frustration and anger

A sense of being imprisoned, trapped, impotent is often reported by dyslexic adults. George, a long-distance lorry driver, describes it thus:

> I felt I couldn't move in any direction. In my job I was always moving, going in all directions, but in myself I couldn't go anywhere. I was grounded. That's why I liked the driving – I would drive and drive and drive to try and get away from the frustration, but however far you drive, you can't get away from yourself.

In human beings, frustration soon turns to anger. For a child, frustration is a very common experience, and a child's anger often has a specific target: the parent, the teacher, some particular adult, or perhaps a sibling, who is perceived as frustrating the child's needs.

For an adult, the situation may be more complex. In the case of a dyslexic adult who feels immense frustration at his inability to progress in his studies or in his work as he feels he should, who should his anger be directed against? Who is causing him the frustration? Can he blame his tutor for failing him in an exam when he knows he did not finish the paper? Can he blame his boss for not promoting him when he feels incompetent to do even his present job? Can he blame his parents for somehow failing to bring him up properly? Or his teachers for not recognizing his problems? How can he pinpoint where the failure lay?

In fact, all too often a dyslexic adult ends up being angry with himself.

Or he feels an impotent anger against some impenetrable Fate or Destiny, which, for reasons unknown, has blighted his life.

Victor, who struggled for years with low self-esteem and frustration at not being able to make progress in his career, writes as follows:

> I have to say that I am a lot calmer than I was two years ago, I have a strong feeling that I would have ended up killing someone, just to get some of the frustration out of myself, who it would have been I don't know, it would very probably just have been simply someone at random. When I went for an assessment it was the best thing I ever did, I can't describe the relief I felt when the psychologist explained I was dyslexic. I don't know what I would have done if I hadn't found out.

Anxiety, fear and panic

Whatever difficulties one may have in life, anxiety usually makes them worse, and this is certainly true of dyslexic difficulties. Adult dyslexics have spent years worrying about their ability to perform certain tasks, worrying about whether they can manage an academic course or hold down a job. Often, as Deirdre wrote above, they feel an acute anxiety about being 'found out'. In the end, the anxiety about the difficulties is as much of the problem as the difficulties themselves. A vicious circle of anxiety and inefficiency is created from which there seems no escape.

Of course, anxiety and stress can also precipitate physical symptoms: nausea, migraine, susceptibility to viral infections, and to more serious illness. Being physically below par naturally further reduces efficiency and so the downward spiral continues.

Sometimes anxiety intensifies into fear, even panic attacks. Hugo, who was an executive in a large advertising company, knew that he had dyslexic difficulties and had indeed discussed them with his employers, who were sympathetic. Nonetheless, he lived in a state of constant anxiety that he would be unable to manage his work or that he would miss deadlines and let people down, perhaps be responsible for losing a client. A nagging feeling of anxiety had become a way of life for him: it was an everyday companion and he could no longer imagine life without it. He assumed it was the cross he had to bear, that he would continue in this way indefinitely, muddling on somehow.

But things got worse: he began to experience attacks of panic, sometimes in the morning as he was dressing for work, sometimes on the tube on his journey to the office, sometimes – which was worst of all – at the office itself when he was dealing with clients or meeting with colleagues. The attack always started in the same way: his heart began to thump, his hands felt clammy, and he lost the immediate sense of his surroundings. He felt that he must be having a heart attack, that he was going to die, and, although the attacks began to recur frequently, and he suffered no physical harm, each time one occurred the terror of annihilation was just as great. He thought he must be going mad, cracking up, going to pieces. He felt unable to tell anybody about the attacks, assuming that they would think he was crazy. He felt that life was disintegrating around him, that he was going to lose everything and spend the remainder of his days locked away in some institution which catered for the insane.

Eventually the situation became so bad that he was unable to go to work at all. In a way, this worsening of the situation proved his salvation. He was forced to visit his doctor and to give some account of what had been happening to him. What had seemed to Hugo to be a hellish torture and madness, somehow brought on by his own weakness, was regarded in a much more matter-of-fact light by the doctor. Chronic stress and panic attacks was the diagnosis and appropriate treatment was arranged with a clinical psychologist at the local hospital. Hugo was soon able to resume his working life and, though it was several months before the worst of the panic attacks subsided, he was able, with help and support from the psychologist, to develop a better understanding of what was happening to him, both mentally and physically, when such attacks occurred, and to develop strategies of coping with the situation.

Despondency, depression and despair

Veena's story:

> I'm 32 years old now, living happily with my partner and our small son. I work part time at a local play group and enjoy my work very much. I've got lots of interests – in particular I like music and outdoor activities. So, yes, now life is very good. People tell me I'm lucky, and I think, yes, I am, but I don't tell them that only two years ago I was so depressed about myself I didn't care whether I lived or died.
>
> I thought back to try and remember when it was that I started feeling miserable about myself but I can't really remember the beginning of it. It seems as if as a child I always was miserable. And it wasn't because we were an unhappy family, nothing like that, we were quite jolly and cosy at home and I just took it for granted that my parents loved me.
>
> I think it was more at school that I used to feel wretched. I know I used not to want to go to school; as a small kid I'm told I had to be dragged

there screaming. My main memory of school is sitting rigid at my desk with my head down watching all the children around me busily reading or writing or doing things and feeling that I couldn't. I was usually bottom of the class. I wasn't unpopular at school, though, I think because I was good at sport and I was always wanted on the team. In the end everybody seemed to be happy with saying 'Oh well, she's good at sport' and it was just assumed there was no hope for me academically.

I know I never accepted that though. I know I was quite a quick-thinking child and curious about the world and I wanted to learn, but I couldn't, I was always shut out of it. I felt frustrated, and angry sometimes, but I was a very well-behaved child, that's the way I was brought up – I never made a fuss or showed that I was upset. I just kept sitting there sort of paralysed and wishing the nightmare would end.

I left school at 16 without qualifications, and the first thing that happened was that I lost all my former friends. They stayed on at school and eventually went on to college. They seemed to live in a cheerful and purposeful world that I just didn't belong to. I just kicked around doing temporary jobs but nothing that really interested me.

After a while I seemed to lose interest in anything, and my energy was always low. I found that I was going home in the evening and bursting into tears. I kept sitting around a lot just staring into space and feeling everything was too much effort. I didn't actually think of myself as being depressed in any serious way. After all, everybody gets a bit down sometimes, and I kept assuming that I was tired, working too hard or that it would pass. But it didn't pass. I was preoccupied with gloomy thoughts. As I scanned my life, there seemed to be no part of it which had any direction. I couldn't get any qualifications, I couldn't get a decent job, I had no friends, I couldn't respect myself any more.

I was working as a receptionist, but I lost my job because I kept not turning up for work. Somehow when that happened it made me realize that something really was wrong. I'd always thought of myself as a very responsible and conscientious person and now I could hardly recognize myself any more. Was this person really me?

I started thinking about ending it all. I come from a Roman Catholic background and that sort of thing is thought of as a sin. But I thought we shoot dogs when they're suffering unbearably, why not humans?

I suppose things could have ended otherwise, but life took a turn. It was pure luck. I was chatting one day at church with a woman I knew very slightly and she happened to mention that she had recently been diagnosed dyslexic. As she was describing her difficulties, I thought 'that's me!', and I asked her more about it.

This was the turning point. It was as if somebody had suddenly given me the key that unlocked all the closed doors of my life. It led to me getting some help for my difficulties and was the beginning of a long road that led me out of darkness and back into the light.

Relief, determination and hope

It perhaps seems as if this chapter has been full of gloom and doom. Yet all the emotions that have been described here are commonly reported by dyslexic adults, especially in cases where the difficulties have for a long time not been recognized and understood. It is difficult to go on feeling positive about oneself when one is constantly tripped up, frustrated and humiliated by inexplicable inefficiencies.

However, once dyslexic difficulties have been recognized and strategies for dealing with them put in place, life can often take a turn for the better. All the energy that previously went into worrying about the problems and covering them up can now be channelled into developing effective ways of dealing with them, both practically and emotionally.

Many adults find that simply having an assessment brings an enormous feeling of relief. It means that their 'condition' is not mysterious any longer, it is named, categorized, analysed and – perhaps most of all – recognized.

Although adults often approach an assessment fearing that it will bring them bad news, in fact the opposite is usually the case. This is because an assessment, as well as pinpointing weaknesses, points up areas of ability, and many dyslexic adults feel literally stunned when they see not only their difficulties but also their strengths, often very great, laid before them in black and white.

As was the case with 'Tom' in Chapter 3, when the first surprise or shock wears off, a variety of emotions can follow: elation at having got things sorted out, anger about the years of confusion, grief at the thought of the opportunities that have been lost through lack of understanding of the situation. In the end, however, what usually emerges most strongly is a sense of hope and a feeling of determination.

Victor, whose account of his angry feelings was given above, writes as follows:

The first thing that has to happen is for the dyslexic to accept that they have the condition; once they have done that they can move on. Confidence is built and poor self-image slowly ditched. Also a lot of the frustration has now gone and I am starting to be able to express my creative side. For example, it is only since I discovered that I was dyslexic that I have started

to do marquetry, it is not only very therapeutic it also helps the hand–eye
co-ordination. Once you have discovered you have a condition called
dyslexia, life becomes more comfortable, more relaxed and enjoyable.

Finally, Ingrid, a woman who only discovered that she was dyslexic in her
45th year, describes her feelings thus:

> I felt as if the prison doors had been opened. I looked out and saw paths
> leading in all directions. I didn't know which of the paths was mine. All I
> did know was that I would have a path in future and that the years of
> confinement were over.

Coping with emotions

All the emotions described in this chapter are, of course, felt in certain
situations by all human beings, not just by dyslexic people, and one of
the difficulties in counselling dyslexic adults is knowing, as it were,
where to stop. In practice, there are two main therapeutic approaches:
behaviour/cognitive therapy, which tends to focus on particular feelings
and situations (for example, stress and anxiety felt as a result of
workplace difficulties), and psychodynamic therapy, which is a much
broader, 'no-holds-barred' look at a person's emotional and imaginative
life. Various practical strategies for coping with emotions are considered
in detail in Chapter 16.

Further reading

Miles TR, Varma V (eds) (1995) Dyslexia and Stress. London: Whurr.

PART 2

Tackling the difficulties

Introduction

This part of the book covers ways in which people can deal with their dyslexic difficulties at work – from general work organization to tackling the emotions and negative attitudes that so often accompany dyslexia. Much of the advice applies to dyspraxic, as well as dyslexic, people.

Dyslexic people are not all alike. They are individuals, each with their own individual pattern of dyslexic difficulties and their own preferred learning styles; and each with their own strengths and talents. For this reason, there is a range of different strategies and advice for them to choose from in each chapter.

Wherever possible, there will be techniques that draw on the visual and imaginative skills that many dyslexic people have developed to compensate for their dyslexic difficulties. However, since reading, writing and organization are essentially linear, sequential activities, there are many techniques and strategies to help dyslexic people acquire and develop these very necessary abilities.

As well as covering specific workplace tasks and activities, there is also some general advice and guidance on basic reading, writing and memory skills. There is no point telling a dyslexic person about formal report or memo structures, or telling them to 'plan their reports', without also giving some basic advice on writing flow and structure, and on different ways of planning for written work. And the memory techniques for remembering work documents are essentially the same as those for remembering any written work.

Of course, all this information is presented in the form of a mass of written words, which can be daunting to dyslexic people. (In effect, they are being faced with pages of written text advising them how to read written text, and written instructions telling them how to remember written instructions.) To make things easier for them, they would do well to follow the advice given throughout these chapters of the book – to tackle it one bit at a time.

It is also always easier to learn by active practice and interaction. Dyslexic readers might consider enlisting the co-operation of a friend or colleague to help them practise the various techniques. They might also benefit from some initial face-to-face training or tuition – perhaps a few initial sessions to help them get to grips with the range of advice, and to assess and select techniques most appropriate to them. This would also give them the chance to get some interactive practice and feedback in different areas, to get them started and set them on track.

Chapter 8
Getting started

We have already explored the range of dyslexic difficulties and their assessment in Part 1. The next step is to start to tackle those difficulties – and to many dyslexic people, this step may well feel more daunting than anything they have had to face so far. The assessment is over; they have begun to come to terms with the fact that they have dyslexia; they have already started to deal with the range of conflicting emotions that this knowledge has triggered. But they still feel that they are at the very beginning. They are probably feeling frustration and anger at the wasted years and the lost opportunities; and they now find themselves facing the task of tackling their dyslexic difficulties – and all the time and effort that will involve. For this reason there is often a time lapse between a person being diagnosed as dyslexic and their applying for tuition. They need some time to gather their confused emotions together and prepare to face the next step – out of the difficulties that have plagued them all their lives.

The important thing for dyslexic people to recognize at this stage is that there *are* ways to combat their dyslexic difficulties. It will take time and perseverance – how much will depend on the severity of their dyslexia – but they will be able to tackle it. And it may well not be as difficult as they feared. Like so many things, the starting is often the hardest part.

Usually, tackling dyslexic difficulties will involve a three-pronged attack for dyslexic adults. First, they will need to learn strategies and techniques to help counteract the underlying dyslexic difficulties themselves. These may include multi-sensory memory and planning techniques; organizational strategies; more efficient methods of working; and the use of visual techniques to help tackle a range of different tasks.

Second, they will probably have to catch up on basic reading, writing and organizational skills that they may well have failed to acquire, or have fallen behind in, because of their dyslexia. These may include learning some basic rules of spelling, grammar, writing, reading and maths. The training should take account of their dyslexia, and of their own particular learning styles, and provide the specialized help they need to learn these basic skills effectively – and without the torture that was probably involved when they first tried to learn them.

Third, most dyslexic people will need to tackle the mental barriers – the damaging negative attitudes and expectations and the low self-confidence that have built up over the years because of their dyslexia, and that may be hindering their performance almost as much as the dyslexia itself.

Having mentioned mental barriers, it is important for dyslexic people to remember that they have strengths as well as weaknesses - and to acknowledge and use those strengths and talents. Many dyslexic adults will have developed good visual, creative and problem-solving skills to combat their dyslexic difficulties, and these can be put to good use in dealing with their dyslexia.

The following chapters cover ways to tackle dyslexia and improve performance in the specific context of the workplace. They deal with a range of typical workplace tasks and activities, from basic filing and data entry to project planning, time management and organizing the overall workload. They cover various types of writing and reading tasks encountered at work, such as reading and remembering work documents, and planning and writing work documents like memos, business letters, reports and notes of meetings. They include oral skills at work, from interacting with colleagues and making telephone calls to speaking at meetings and making oral presentations. They also cover ways to tackle mental barriers, such as lack of confidence, anxiety and stress. Finally, they look at ways that dyslexic workers can tell their employers and work colleagues about their dyslexia, and present a list of guidelines for employers on ways they can help – and not hinder – dyslexic employees.

As newly diagnosed dyslexic adults stand at the brink of beginning to tackle their dyslexic difficulties at work, it is perhaps a good time for them to remember that dyslexia has nothing to do with underlying intelligence, talent and ability. They should never confuse dyslexia with these – and never let others do it.

Now that they know it is dyslexia that has held them back, they should remember not to let it stop them from aiming for what they really want to do – if they feel they possess the underlying talent. Of course tackling the dyslexia will not miraculously produce talents they do not have. And of course it will take time and effort to combat the dyslexia and build up their work skills. But once they start, and begin to move forward step by step, they will certainly be able to achieve much more than they ever thought they could. Slowly but surely, tackling the dyslexic difficulties will free them to express the talents they already have, and to fulfill their underlying potential.

Chapter 9
Overall work strategies

Throughout the following chapters there are several common themes: overall strategies and general advice that apply to a wide range of different tasks and activities. These general strategies will help dyslexic employees to cope more easily and efficiently with most types of work – from carrying out specific tasks to managing their overall workload. In effect, they will help workers to feel in control of their workload, rather than feeling overwhelmed by it. This chapter provides an introduction to each of these recurring themes.

Planning and preparing: taking control and seeing the 'whole'

It is an all too common fault to feel that there is not enough time to plan – particularly for people who have dyslexic difficulties, which make everything take so much longer to do. The truth is that there is not enough time *not* to plan – and this is even more important for those who have to contend with the typical dyslexic difficulties in sequencing and short-term memory.

Most people would not dream of going on holiday, for example, without some degree of planning (booking ahead, applying for leave, making lists of essential items to take). Yet those same people will often attempt to write complex reports, carry out detailed tasks or get through a heavy working week without any planning at all.

Planning and preparation are, quite simply, thinking ahead – and thinking of the whole activity. Without forward-thinking, and without getting an overview of the whole task, it is all too easy to make mistakes, to forget important things and to lose control of a task. An unplanned letter will probably be muddled and difficult to understand, and may well fail to include an essential point or two. An unplanned day will probably result in too much time being spent on one task to the detriment of others, and perhaps some missed appointments or deadlines. An unplanned task will no doubt be completed in the end – but far less efficiently, far more slowly and probably far more stressfully than a planned task.

With dyslexia, it is all too easy to miss out important steps or sections – or to get them out of order, making an activity less efficient, or a letter less easy for the reader to follow. To prevent this happening, it is essential for dyslexic people to take the time to stand back and plan for everything – the task, the meeting, the day, the week, even the ten-minute talk with a boss or colleague. Planning means stopping to take a full look at the whole activity, or the whole week or month, before actually starting to tackle it bit by bit. This enables the person to get a full picture of everything that the task or the week involves – and then to sort each thing into a sensible order, and to allocate enough time and resources for each bit. In effect, it allows workers to feel in control. Now all they have to do is perform the planned steps one at a time.

Of course, with dyslexia, 'performing the planned steps one at a time' may not seem all that easy. However, it will certainly be easier than performing them without planning, or trying to plan and perform at the same time. Knowing that a clear plan has been made – a plan that covers everything that needs to be done, in a reasonable order – will relieve the stress that would exacerbate the dyslexic difficulties. It will free dyslexic workers to concentrate fully on basic skills such as spelling, punctuation or calculating, without having to worry at the same time about the overall structure and shape of the task.

It is important for dyslexic employees to remember that planning will usually save them time. The time spent in planning will generally be more than made up by the greater ease of carrying out the task – and getting it right first time.

Guidelines for specific types of planning for different activities are given in the subsequent chapters.

Breaking things down and working in stages

However clear the plan, the prospect of carrying out the whole project or getting through the entire week will probably seem daunting to the dyslexic employee. Now is the time to focus on the smaller bits or stages – and to tackle them one piece at a time. This advice is another recurring theme throughout the following chapters.

Having dyslexia often makes it hard to concentrate on one thing at a time. Dyslexic people may find their minds leaping from one idea to another, veering off the point and leaving them in a muddle. To fight this tendency, it helps to break tasks down into bits, and then focus on each bit separately.

Dyslexic employees will find that most tasks and activities will seem much easier, and less daunting, if they are broken down into manageable chunks or small stages. (If they cannot face a five-mile run, then they could run for half a mile, stop for a sandwich, run another half mile, and so on.) Again, this applies to many different things – the project, the task, the report, the day. If there is a long report to read, it can be taken one section – or even one page – at a time; a letter can be written one paragraph, or one subsection of the plan, at a time. And the day, once planned out, can be taken one hour at a time, or one task at a time.

Once an activity has been split into chunks, it often helps to see the chunks as subgoals set for each task. It also helps to write the subgoals down and tick off each one as it is completed. This allows dyslexic employees to monitor their progress and to get a feeling of movement and achievement. Crossing off the subgoals can also be a powerful motivator – urging people on to cross off more and more chunks of work, one by one. In effect, their plan and their subgoals work together – the former giving an organized overview of the whole thing, and the latter providing a step-by-step progression through the separate stages.

Getting help

The next familiar theme that crops up again and again in the following chapters is the advice to dyslexic workers to get whatever help they can – from their workmates, their supervisors, their company, and even their clients or customers.

Many dyslexic employees feel embarrassed about asking for help – or even admitting to their employer or work colleagues that they have dyslexia. (This latter point is covered in greater detail in Chapter 17.) But there are many ways in which colleagues and employers will be able to help them. They should take advantage of all the help they can get, with confidence and assertiveness. Simple things such as getting permission to tape a talk or asking for better layout of documents can make a great difference to performance. If they are asked, employers will also probably be happy – or at least willing – to help their dyslexic staff plan their jobs or organize their work schedules.

Dyslexic people should also note that getting help from their employer is now a right, not a favour. (See Chapter 20 on the Disability Discrimination Act.)

Of course, it is not only people who can help. Dyslexic staff should also request and take full advantage of the wide range of equipment that can make their job easier and quicker, from voice mail and voice dictation systems to tape recorders and electronic diaries. There is even a pen that will read out words, break them into syllables and define them when it is scanned over the words.

Various ways in which employers can help are referred to in more detail in relation to specific tasks, and covered fully in Chapter 18.

Taking breaks

Another piece of advice that applies to all types of work is the advice to take regular short breaks to refresh concentration and so improve performance. In any office, there is usually one person with his head down for the entire day, and another who appears always to be having a coffee break. It may be surprising to find that the coffee drinker's output at the end of the day is probably considerably higher – but research has shown that this is very likely to be the case. Performance and output tend to get progressively worse over time unless regular brief breaks are taken. After a whole morning without breaks, workers' heads may be down, but so will their output.

People tend to work most efficiently if they notice the point at which their concentration begins to decline and take a brief break at that stage. Overall, they will accomplish more – not less – if they take breaks. Dyslexic people should try to think of breaks not as wasted time, but as valuable time to 'recharge their batteries'. The breaks will enable them to work all the time on full capacity, rather than struggling along on steadily flagging batteries, accomplishing less and less as time goes on. If they are not able to take breaks, they should try alternating tasks when their concentration flags.

Taking it slowly

An important piece of general advice is to take things slowly. It is the old familiar cliché of 'more haste less speed'. Surprising though it may seem, many dyslexic people are prone to dive blindly into tasks without thinking. For some of them, it is because they feel the need to rush into things to make up for the fact that their dyslexia makes their output slower. For some, it is because they want to 'catch' thoughts or ideas before they disappear. And for some, it is because their lack of confidence makes them afraid to appear slow. (For these people, it is worth reflecting that pausing before making an oral reply, or asking for a repetition, usually appears thoughtful or efficient, rather than slow.)

The common result of rushing into tasks is that they come out in a muddle, probably have to be done again and take longer in the end. So it is usually quicker to take the time to think things through – to plan, to consider, to check. Many dyslexic employees have found that going slowly actually means going faster.

Using visual and creative strengths

Nothing is all bad – and dyslexia is no exception. Over the years of battling with their difficulties, dyslexic people will inevitably and automatically (often unconsciously) have built up a range of compensatory strengths and strategies.

To compensate for their dyslexic difficulties, many dyslexic people develop the right hemisphere of their brain much more strongly than they would have done without the dyslexia. The right hemisphere deals not in words and sequences, but in visual images and overviews. Because of their dyslexia, these people may well have developed strong visual skills which can be put to use in a range of tasks. They are also likely to be creative – able to come up with innovative ideas and original thoughts. As well as being a valuable talent in itself, this creativity can be put to use to help them think their way around some of the problems caused by dyslexia.

Through force of circumstances, dyslexic people often also become masters of strategic skills, through constantly having to devise ways around problems that non-dyslexic people never have to face. These, too, can come in very useful in tackling their dyslexic difficulties.

Although most of this part of the book is devoted to helping people to overcome the difficulties caused by dyslexia, rather than teaching them things they can already do, it also refers to ways they might use their existing visual, creative and strategic talents in different types of work.

Chapter 10
General work organization

People who suffer from dyslexia will be well aware of the effect that it can have on general organizational skills. Unfortunately, all too few employers are aware of this. It is not uncommon for dyslexic employees to find their jobs on the line because they are unable to gain control of their overall workload, and because their employers put this down to incompetence and disorder. Dyslexic people usually find that the difficulties of work organisation are worst in office work, or at higher levels of responsibility. However, even jobs which may appear on the surface to need fewer organisational skills often turn out to involve quite detailed organisation. Dyslexic people should remember that there are ways to tackle this problem and to put them in control of their work. The following two stories are typical examples.

Ben is an intelligent and sociable man in his mid 30s. He holds down a busy and responsible job in a city investment bank, and has just been promoted. He is well-liked and respected by his colleagues as an efficient and capable professional. Looking at him now, it is hard to believe that just over two years ago, Ben was on the verge of being fired. His latest work assessment report had described him as 'disorganized', 'unmotivated' and 'difficult to get on with'.

Ben's feelings at the time ranged between confusion and frustration, hopelessness and anger. He was working late every night, and taking work home – to the irritation of his family. Yet he was still unable to keep up with his workload. He regularly failed to meet deadlines and forgot to return important telephone calls; his written reports were rejected as muddled, disorganized and verbose; he became short-tempered and withdrawn, and began to clash with his colleagues. Ben did not know that he had dyslexia. But, fortunately for him, a friend who had seen a television documentary on dyslexia suggested that this might be the problem. He had an assessment and was diagnosed dyslexic. After coming to terms with the diagnosis, he launched himself with energy into a course of training to tackle all his dyslexic difficulties – and in particular to build up a range of basic work organizational skills. Ben is now in control of his job, and his employers find it very hard to remember the awkward, disorganized person they were about to fire three years ago.

*   *   *

Algie, a dyslexic chef, had deliberately sought a job in which he would not be hampered by his difficulties. He found his training difficult – but having passed that hurdle, he expected to be able to concentrate on cooking and leave his dyslexic difficulties behind him. His hopes were soon dashed. After an initial period of nothing but cooking, Algie was rewarded for his success by being given responsibility to manage the kitchen. On top of the cooking, he was now responsible for organising the daily running of the kitchen and supervising several trainee chefs. Algie found this very difficult; the restaurant was popular and busy, and he became very confused and muddled trying to keep track of food stocks, make daily orders and plan menus as well as cooking. He was in a constant state of stress trying to juggle the various tasks. Regularly, he would forget to order essential supplies, and he had difficulty matching the menus with the ingredients in stock. He did all his work in a rush and the quality of his cooking deteriorated. He rarely had time to help the trainee chefs, who seemed to be constantly clamouring for his attention and bombarding him with questions. Algie's employer became increasingly concerned about the organisation of her restaurant – and Algie became more and more stressed and unconfident.

Fortunately, Algie's employer valued his cooking talents sufficiently to want to keep him on. To help him get in control of his work, she decided to send him for some training in work organisation. He learned how to structure his shifts to incorporate set times for planning menus, checking stock and making food orders, and he learned more efficient ways to carry out these tasks. He learned how to set up a series of 'action lists' to record stocks that were running low and ingredients that were needed for the following day's menus. He incorporated these into an 'action board' on the wall, where he could note things as they arose. He also learned techniques to help reduce stress and anxiety and to build up his confidence. It took some time, but Algie is now in control of his workload, as well as producing very good food. He is beginning to feel confident enough to consider setting up and managing a restaurant of his own.

Acquiring good work organizational skills is important for everyone, but for people who have dyslexia, it is essential. They need to organize their work space and plan their time. They need to set up a system to keep them in control of their total workload – to make them aware of all aspects of their job, and to keep track of their progress. They need planned daily, weekly and monthly work schedules, with the flexibility to encompass unexpected tasks and interruptions. And they need techniques to plan and carry out larger tasks and long-term projects.

Managing time and tasks

It is very common, with dyslexia, to miss appointments and deadlines, lose track of tasks and confuse priorities. This leaves dyslexic workers feeling out of control and causes stress, which exacerbates their dyslexic difficulties, causing further stress, and so on. To escape from this vicious circle, it is important for them to stand back, take a look at everything their job involves, and then set up a clear and simple system of recording and routinely checking all they have to do, and allocating slots of time in the day to do it.

The following process of organisation may well appear daunting and difficult to put into effect. Dyslexic employees are advised to get whatever help and guidance they can from bosses, work colleagues or friends to help them set the process in motion. To make it all seem more manageable, they could think of it as four separate activities to be carried out one at a time.

1. Building up an overview of the total workload.
2. Breaking it down into separate tasks, goals and sub-goals.
3. Recording all the tasks and goals.
4. Daily monitoring of progress, and up-dating of action lists.

Materials

Before starting, it helps to choose the materials that will be needed to record activities and to check progress.

Diaries and calendars

Most employees will need a diary, a calendar and perhaps (depending on their job) a year-planner to give them an instant, long-term overview. They should choose diaries and calendars with good, clear layout and sufficient space. They should also explore the use of electronic and computer diaries and calendars, and choose the method that they feel most comfortable with.

Action lists

They will also need to design action lists – again with good layout, and perhaps incorporating separate columns or sections for urgent and less urgent work, and for routine daily or weekly tasks. Again, people should consider using computer action lists if this is more appealing to them.

For complex jobs with long-term projects, it may be easier to use several action lists – one for current jobs, with urgent work highlighted; one for routine work; and one for longer-term tasks. This will allow the current action list to be replaced when it becomes full, without having to rewrite all the long-term and routine tasks at the same time.

All action lists and calendars should be kept in a place where they can be seen easily – on a wall or notice board, or in a coloured folder. (Printing or copying the action lists on coloured paper can help to make them easily noticeable.)

Getting an overview

Once they have got their materials ready, dyslexic workers may well be wondering where on earth to start, and how to get all their activities, appointments, meetings and tasks recorded and prioritized. At the outset, they will have to take some time to look at and analyse all aspects of their job and everything on their plate at present. They should think of this as the initial planning stage – the stage when they take control, by getting an overview of the whole job before breaking it down into bits and stages.

It may well be necessary to set aside a whole afternoon or a whole day to do this - but organization is an essential part of any job. If necessary, employees should inform their boss that this is what they are doing, and remember that he or she is more likely to be impressed by their efficiency than to see them as wasting time. If the job really is too hectic to find the time, it is well worth staying late one evening, or coming in for one weekend day. (This initial planning should be only a one-off task – *provided people remember to check and update their lists and diaries every day from then on.*)

Master list

To build up the overview, employees need to pull together all their old lists and diaries, check through papers and files on their desk and make a

Master List of all outstanding tasks (from the largest project to the briefest telephone call), and all appointments and meetings. They should think of anything they need to do to prepare for appointments and meetings, and add these to the tasks already on their Master List. It is important to remember to include all routine daily, weekly or monthly duties, for example reading the post, daily filing, monthly accounts deadlines, etc.

Of course, remembering all tasks and appointments – and making a list of them – is not at all easy for many dyslexic people. It may help if they record everything in a visual format at first, for example in the form of a spider diagram or flow chart, before compiling their Master List. They might also consider enlisting their boss, or a work colleague, at this stage to help them build up a clear and complete picture of everything on their plate. They could even ask a friend to help – as simply talking through a job with someone else should help to jog the memory.

At the end of all this listing, dyslexic employees may feel a bit overwhelmed at the size of the list of work before them. But they have reached the crucial point where they can now see the whole thing, and feel reasonably confident that everything is there.

Breaking down and recording work

The next step is to take the whole and break it down into different types of work, varying degrees of urgency and – for larger tasks – smaller stages. This could be done by simply writing coloured code letters beside items on the Master List, for example a red star beside urgent tasks, a blue 'R' for routine tasks and a purple 'P' for projects. Then it is ready to be recorded in diaries, calendars and action lists.

With dyslexia, it is easy for people to lose track of where they are in a job, so they need to work systematically, starting at the top of their Master List and recording each action, one by one, in the appropriate diary, calendar or action list, crossing out each item as they record it. It will be easier to deal with the different entries separately – first the diary entries, then the calendar and then the action lists.

First, go through the Master List from top to bottom, recording all appointments, meetings and deadlines on the calendar, crossing them off the Master List as they are entered.

Second, copy each calendar entry into the diary. Now only the tasks for the action list will remain uncrossed off.

Third, go through the Master List again, copying each task on to the action lists. Enter the tasks that need to be done soon on the **'current'**

action list; enter the regular daily or weekly tasks on the '**routine**' **action list**; and enter the non-urgent tasks on the '**long-term**' **action list**. (Long tasks or projects should be broken up into stages, with each stage entered as a separate task. There are more details on this later.)

It is important to take the time to write the tasks clearly and legibly, with spaces or lines between each task (see Figure 1). A squashed, scrawled action list is difficult to follow – and could prevent you from noticing every task. Many dyslexic people also find it helpful to write out their lists on coloured paper that stands out among a pile of other papers, and to use colours and highlights to make the list easier to read. When tasks become urgent, they can be starred, circled or highlighted on the action list.

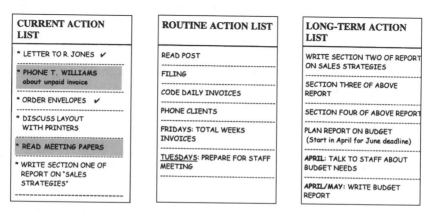

Figure 1: Examples of action lists

Of course, it is not possible in a book of this nature to list all the numerous details that constitute everything that needs to be done in any one specific job. Dyslexic employees might find it of benefit in the initial stages to get expert assistance to help them break up their overall workload and organize it into daily and weekly schedules.

Taking control

Dyslexic employees should now have the full picture of their work, their deadlines and their appointments – all recorded on calendar, diary and action lists. The whole workload may well seem daunting, but seeing it as a whole puts them in control. They will have no more nagging doubts about whether there is something important that they have completely forgotten about. They can see clearly what is urgent and needs to be tackled first.

Seeing their entire workload listed out also serves to alert dyslexic workers if there really is too much to handle, and provides them with the evidence of this fact. If there is too much to cope with, this is the time to take control by discussing any clashing priorities with their boss and deciding which should take precedence, or getting in extra help to tackle the load.

Having made themselves aware of the whole, it is time once again to shift focus to concentrate on the bits, and to progress steadily through them, one at a time. Taking one thing at a time, workers should choose an urgent task from their action lists, start work on it and cross it off when they have done it.

Staying in control: regular monitoring of lists

Building up the full picture of all the work is, of course, only the starting point. It is all too easy to make lists and then fail to read them. To stay in control, it will be necessary to set up a **routine monitoring system** – and to develop the habit of entering each new task or appointment in the appropriate place as soon as it arises.

First, it helps to set some **routine 'checkpoints'** every day – times to review and update action lists and calendars – for example, first thing in the morning, midday and the end of the day. These checkpoints will serve several purposes:

- they remind people what they have to do
- they allow them to monitor their progress
- they allow them to prepare for the day and week ahead
- they also serve as motivators, by giving a satisfying feeling of achievement as each completed task is crossed off.

With dyslexia, it is common to read a list and then forget what is on it, so this regular checking of action lists is particularly important.

A typical checking routine might be:

First thing in the morning:

- check calendar and diary for any meetings, appointments and deadlines
- check action list for tasks to be done.

Before lunch:

- check calendar and action list again as a reminder
- cross off any jobs completed during the morning.

At the end of the day:

- cross off jobs completed in the afternoon
- make sure to enter all new jobs, meetings, etc., that have arisen during the day
- check actions, deadlines and appointments for the next day, and make any necessary preparations (for example, collecting together papers for a morning meeting; taking home papers if there is a meeting out of the office the next morning)
- note any urgent tasks not completed, and highlight them on the action list
- copy any new appointments from diary to calendar, and vice versa.

At the end of each week:

- check calendar and action lists for the week ahead
- note any actions needed to prepare for next week's meetings or appointments, and add them to current action list
- look at the long-term action list, and copy tasks from there on to the current action list as appropriate.

Regularly:

- establish the habit of writing new tasks, deadlines or appointments on action lists or the calendar as soon as they arise
- when an action list fills up, copy all uncompleted tasks on to a new blank action list
- whenever a big task comes in, break it into smaller tasks and enter each of these as separate tasks on the appropriate action lists, with deadlines in the calendar.

Planning the day

As previously mentioned, a common problem with dyslexia is the tendency to dart from one job to another and back, rather than completing one job at a time. This is partly due to the difficulty of keeping attention focused on one thing, and partly due to difficulties with prioritizing. Whatever the reason, it is not an efficient way to work – and it provides little motivation or satisfaction, as no one job is finished, and people are faced with a complex and untidy pile of half-finished jobs.

To help tackle this problem, it may be helpful (if the job allows it) to plan a daily work routine, allocating chunks of time to particular jobs or to similar types of work. This will enable dyslexic employees to get into the flow of one job or type of work, and thus to progress faster and more efficiently. In effect, having broken their total workload down into bits, they will now be doing the same to their day.

Of course it is not easy to plan the day in a job where unplanned work crops up and interruptions occur frequently. However, a daily plan can include slots of 'free time' to incorporate unexpected tasks. And simply having an 'ideal day' to stick to whenever possible will help to give structure to the day and improve performance.

Some people might decide, for example, to spend the first hour of the day reading and sorting the post and doing some filing. The next hour might be allocated to phone calls to clients or customers. After a coffee break, the two hours before lunch might be spent doing written work – letters, memos, e-mails, or reports.

After lunch, they might set aside a 'free' hour to absorb any unexpected tasks that arose during the morning, or to finish off any of the morning's work that took longer to do than they expected. They might then devote half an hour to reading papers and then, after a tea-break, another slot of time for written work.

In a different job, they might allocate slots of time to particular jobs or types of work, such as invoices, calculations, expenses, etc. Or, in a secretarial job, slots of time devoted to typing, photocopying, filing, etc.

Whatever their job, it is important for dyslexic employees to remember to check the action lists and calendar at the beginning, middle and end of every day.

In practice, it will not always be possible to stick to the plan, but dyslexic employees should try to do so whenever possible, and remember that they have the 'free' slot to absorb unplanned tasks. If a job is too unpredictable to allow such planning, people should at least try as often as possible to finish one task before beginning another, and try to do similar types of work together to allow them to build up flow and speed.

Some general guidelines for planning the day

1 Write down a daily plan, and keep it where it can be seen.
2 Include short breaks in the plan, as these help to increase output and improve efficiency.
3 Try to alternate between different types of work, for example an hour of work requiring heavy concentration followed by an hour of easier work.
4 Allocate work that requires strong concentration to the time of day when the brain is most alert.
5 Remember to include the 'checkpoints' in the daily plan.
6 Be flexible: if people feel in the mood to do something different from

the plan, they should do it, but remember to note what they have not done, and do it later in the day.

Example of daily plan

9.00–9.10:	Checkpoint 1 – Check action lists
9.10–10.00:	Post and filing
10.00–10.30:	Make phone calls
10.30–10.45:	Coffee break
10.45–12.00:	Write reports
12.00–12.10:	Take short break (or discuss work with colleagues)
12.10–12.50:	Phone calls
12.50–1.00:	Checkpoint 2 – Check action lists, cross out and add tasks
1.00–2.00:	Lunch
2.00–3.00:	Write letters, memos, e-mails
3.00–3.30:	Discussions with work colleagues
3.30–3.45:	Tea break
3.45–4.45:	Time set aside for unexpected or unfinished tasks
4.45–5.00:	Checkpoint 3 – Add and cross off tasks on action lists. Prepare for tomorrow. On Fridays, prepare for the week ahead.

Organizing work space

After the lists have been made, the calendars filled in, the checking system set up and the day planned, it is time to get down to the work. But dyslexic employees may well find themselves faced with a cluttered desk heaped high with unorganized piles of papers and files. This is confusing at the best of times, but for dyslexic people, it may well make them feel like freezing up completely. If they take the time to sort out their papers, they will find that their mind will feel clearer and they will feel much more in control.

It is not simply a matter of tidying, but also of sorting and categorizing the papers and files into different tasks, types of work and levels of urgency. Once again, the initial sorting out may require a large chunk of time, but the result will be well worth it in terms of efficiency and control.

As with all tasks, if people have dyslexia, it is easy to lose track of where they are. So they should tackle the tidying and sorting methodically and systematically – one thing at a time.

1 Remove any unneeded or outdated items, and consign them to the filing cabinet or the wastepaper basket.
2 Get some folders and desk trays in a range of colours.
3 Collect together papers relating to each separate task, put them in their own folder and label the folder clearly. (Use different coloured folders for different types of work.)
4 Clearly label some desk trays (e.g. 'Urgent', 'Soon', 'Filing', 'To Read', 'Correspondence', 'Invoices').
5 Go through all papers and folders, and sort them into the relevant trays.
6 Double-check that each task in the trays and folders is written on the action lists.
7 Whenever a new task arises, put the papers in the appropriate folder and desk tray (and enter the task on the relevant action list).
8 Put the action lists and calendar on the wall or on a noticeboard, or keep them in a brightly coloured folder in a prominent place.

The results of getting organized

All this organizing and tidying will be time-consuming, and dyslexic people may be wondering whether it is worth the effort. But they will soon see that it has many advantages.

- They will have a tidy desk with all their jobs separated and prioritized, which will help to reduce confusion and enable them to think more clearly.
- They will have all their work listed and prioritized and all their appointments recorded, which is particularly important, given the memory difficulties that dyslexia can cause.
- All of this puts them in control. They know exactly what they have to do, and when they have to do it, and they know where the papers are for each job.
- The feeling of control relieves stress and confusion, which helps people to think more clearly and perform more efficiently.
- If workers find there is too much to do, they have the evidence, and can talk to their boss with confidence about getting help.
- The process of working steadily through each task on their action lists and crossing off completed tasks provides workers with feedback on

their progress. It gives them a sense of achievement, which acts as a motivator to do more.

Finally, it is important for dyslexic employees to remember that all this initial work of listing, proritizing and tidying is a one-off job. But the feeling of control and the resulting improvement in their efficiency will last for as long as they remember to spend a little time each day keeping the system up to date.

Chapter 11
Efficient work methods

The effects of dyslexia on work organisation extend beyond the overall organisational skills covered in the previous chapter. They can also affect the way people carry out specific workplace tasks. Dyslexia can cause people to 'lose their way' in tasks and to use inefficient and time-consuming methods of working. Dyslexic employees may approach tasks in a disorganised manner, moving back and forth between one aspect and another. This tends to slow down progress and reduce accuracy and efficiency.

Dyslexic people in a wide range of different jobs have found that their dyslexic difficulties have hampered their efficiency in carrying out specific tasks – for example, the postman who has to sort letters, the shopkeeper who has to give out correct change, or the manager who has to plan and carry out large projects. However, the area in which dyslexic workers have the most problems is office work – because it combines task organisation with writing and reading skills. Whether they are working on filing, figures or phone calls, doing clerical or administrative work, or planning projects, dyslexic people will find that the sequencing and short-term memory difficulties associated with dyslexia can hamper their efficiency and slow them down. On top of this, many jobs involve overload and pressure, either routinely or from time to time. And when the stress caused by overload is added to the dyslexic difficulties, coping with the daily workload can become overwhelming for dyslexic employees.

This does *not* mean, however, that dyslexic workers cannot do certain tasks. All they need is appropriate help to tackle their difficulties, to learn efficient work techniques, and to harness their strengths. Given this help, they can begin to cope, and to meet all the requirements of their jobs. This chapter covers a range of specific types of work, and looks at ways in which dyslexic employees can improve their speed and efficiency. Whatever the task, they should remember the overall strategies outlined in Chapter 9, which apply to most jobs, big or small: planning; breaking down into stages; working one step at a time; and using their strengths.

General clerical tasks

The following case study illustrates some of the problems that dyslexic employees often encounter in clerical work, and a number of solutions. It describes some work methods that can be applied to a variety of clerical tasks to help counteract the effects of dyslexia.

> Janet, an accounts clerk in a busy department, came to me for training in work skills because she was unable to keep up with the heavy load of routine weekly invoices she had to process in her job. She had been diagnosed as dyslexic, but as yet had done nothing to tackle it. However, as her workload increased, she had begun to feel overwhelmed by the routine coding, calculating and sorting involved in her job. In spite of working long hours of overtime, she was regularly failing to meet her weekly deadlines and was being criticized not only by her own boss but also by the other departments that depended on her work. Her self-confidence had plummeted and she was on the verge of giving up and handing in her notice. She had not told her employers about her dyslexia because she feared it would only increase their lack of confidence in her ability.

The problems

> When we examined Janet's work methods, it was clear that she was tackling her job in a disorganized and inefficient way. She would take a single invoice and painstakingly look up the expenditure code from a long, tightly packed list. Next she would take her calculator and add the amounts, then calculate VAT, then add it on. Then she would go through the whole process again for the second invoice, and so on. When she had 20 invoices, she would batch them together and add up the batch total. Not surprisingly, with her constant moving between coding, calculating, etc., she never got into a flow of work; her concentration was frequently distracted, her calculations often wrong, and her progress slow.

Solutions

> The first part of the solution tackled the difficulty that dyslexic people have with reading complex lists. The expenditure code-list had the worst possible layout for someone with dyslexia – rows and rows of tightly packed, small print. We took some time to mark the list with lines and colours to make it easier to follow: a horizontal line every three rows to help her keep her place; red letters in the margin where each letter of the

alphabet began; highlights on the codes; and circles around the codes most frequently used. As soon as she had time, Janet retyped the code list in a larger, clearer typeface in double spacing with the codes in bold.

The production of a good, clear layout with spaces and colours immediately increased Janet's speed and accuracy in the coding aspect of her job. Before long, everyone else in the department had asked for a copy.

The next part of the solution was to look at Janet's whole job and identify each separate activity that it involved, and to work out the most efficient way of working. The task involved six different actions: coding, adding amounts, calculating VAT, totalling, batching, and adding batch totals. Instead of doing each invoice separately, constantly changing between different activities, Janet simply began to complete each activity separately for all the invoices – all the coding together, then all the adding, then all the VAT, etc. Doing each different activity in one burst enabled her to get into a flow, which improved both her efficiency and her concentration. As a result, her speed and accuracy improved dramatically. She also began to experience a feeling of progress and achievement as she completed each stage and moved on to the next, which motivated her to carry on. Finally, she further enhanced her performance by remembering to take short breaks every hour or so whenever her concentration began to flag.

Before long, Janet was working normal hours, getting all her work done on time, and was ready to take on other work, which she planned and broke down in the same way.

To sum up, the simple strategies that Janet used to help counteract her dyslexic difficulties were:

* improving the layout of complex lists
* taking a look at the whole job and breaking the job down into different activities
* performing each activity separately (grouping similar types of work together)
* progressing systematically through the activities, one at a time
* taking regular short breaks.

These simple strategies can be applied to most clerical and administrative tasks to increase speed and efficiency.

Data entry and copying

Reading, copying and entering figures or text can be a particularly difficult task for dyslexic employees. The dyslexic difficulties make it hard to
keep track of figures and hinder accuracy of copying. However, there are
some very simple things they can do to make the work easier and
improve their accuracy.

Presentation and layout

It is very difficult for anyone to copy data quickly or accurately from
dense, unstructured text, whether on paper or on computer screen. It is
hard to find the place, and there are no subdivisions to serve as markers
or subgoals. In contrast, text that is well-structured (with spaces,
columns, subsections and subheadings, indents and emboldened
sections) is far easier to read, to remember and to copy accurately. The
use of colour also makes things easier to read, either as highlights on
paper, or text and background colours on a computer screen.

The clear presentation and subdivision of text improves the accuracy
and speed of data entry and copying in a number of ways.

- It helps people to keep their place in the text.
- It provides a logical sequence of separate sections, which helps them
  make sense of the material and thus aids memory.
- It provides motivation and gives a sense of progress, by enabling people
  to work through the sections, one by one, as a series of subgoals.
- It stimulates the right side of the brain (particularly if boxes, patterns
  and colours are used). Research has shown that working with both
  sides of the brain together enhances all areas of mental performance.

If the material being copied is not clearly and attractively presented and
structured, dyslexic people can divide and mark it themselves before
copying or entering it. They should remember that although the task of
marking the text will take a little extra time, this time will be small
compared to the time they will save in the subsequent entering of the text.

Copying from clearly marked material will substantially increase the
speed of working. It will also enhance accuracy and avoid time-
consuming corrections. Furthermore, the actual exercise of marking the
text will make people think about it and concentrate on it, both of which
will improve their memory and therefore increase their accuracy.

Texts on paper or computer screens can be marked using highlights,
different colours and different shapes (e.g. boxes, circles, wavy underlines). There are various, specific ways to mark text to make it easier to
remember and copy.

Divide lists of numbers into columns and rows:

- Rule vertical lines between each single column of numbers.
- Rule horizontal lines under every third row of figures. (Three-row chunks tend to be the easiest to work with. With three rows, they are always on the 'beginning', 'middle' or 'end' row of the chunk – all of which are easy to distinguish.
- Tick off each chunk of figures created by the ruled lines, as soon as they have been copied or entered to mark the place and to provide a measure of progress.

2357	3875	8763	9853	974	335	4507
447	1586	763	5983	3896	4509	569
3098	581	3097	7120	609	9561	2650
3397	5408	442	9662	3298	5987	430
507	3901	5973	6872	5772	284	5882
3997	4721	9278	38	1874	4974	3097
298	2047	7927	5175	449	6916	448
6930	2885	1089	330	47	8773	9874
8759	4105	879	2884	9375	3860	8567

2357	3875	8763	9853	974	335	4507
447	1586	763	5983	3896	4509	569
3098	581	3097	7120	609	9561	2650
3397	5408	442	9662	3298	5987	430
507	3901	5973	6872	5772	284	5882
3997	4721	9278	38	1874	4974	3097
298	2047	7927	5175	449	6916	448
6930	2885	1089	330	47	8773	9874
8759	4105	879	2884	9375	3860	8567

Figure 2: Subdivision of numbers

Break up long numbers

Draw horizontal slashes to break down long numbers into several smaller chunks of two or three numbers. The brain can remember a series of chunks far more easily than one long string of figures.

Look for easy-to-remember chunks within long numbers, and divide the number around these.

- 9412368 = 94/123/68

- 70749533 = 707/495/33

- 06500294 = 06/500/294

- 495051 = 49/50/51.

Divide text into sections

Draw lines or boxes to divide the text into sections, and highlight certain bits of information such as dates, reference numbers or totals.

Once they have marked the text in this way, it is easier for dyslexic people if they establish a set pattern for the order in which they copy or enter it. They can use numbers or arrows to link the sections of text in the correct order. Figures 3 and 4 illustrate the difference between a marked and an unmarked invoice.

INVOICE		
To: Shah and Partners 176 High Street Southwood Glasgow	Date: 21 June 2000 Invoice no: 6727	

DESCRIPTION	Unit Price	Total Price
12 Lever Arch files	£5.99	£71.88
5 boxes photocopying paper	£4.50	£22.50
10 boxes of ballpoint pens (blue)	£1.99	£19.90
10 boxes of ballpoint pens (black)	£1.99	£19.90
10 boxes of ballpoint pens (red)	£1.99	£19.90
20 cardboard folders (pink)	£0.75	£15.00
20 cardboard folders (yellow)	£0.75	£15.00
20 cardboard folders (beige)	£0.75	£15.00
20 cardboard folders (orange)	£0.75	£15.00
2 Laser printer toners	£35.00	£70.00
6 rolls Sellotape	£1.20	£7.20
Sub total		**£291.28**
VAT		**£50.97**
Delivery and packing		**£10.00**
Total		**£352.25**

Figure 3: Unmarked invoice

INVOICE		
To: Shah and Partners 176 High Street Southwood Glasgow	Date: 21 June 2000 Invoice no: 6727	

DESCRIPTION	Unit Price	Total Price
12 Lever Arch files	£5.99	£71.88
5 boxes photocopying paper	£4.50	£22.50
10 boxes of ballpoint pens (blue)	£1.99	£19.90
10 boxes of ballpoint pens (black)	£1.99	£19.90
10 boxes of ballpoint pens (red)	£1.99	£19.90
20 cardboard folders (pink)	£0.75	£15.00
20 cardboard folders (yellow)	£0.75	£15.00
20 cardboard folders (beige)	£0.75	£15.00
20 cardboard folders (orange)	£0.75	£15.00
2 Laser printer toners	£35.00	£70.00
6 rolls Sellotape	£1.20	£7.20
Sub total		**£291.28**
VAT		**£50.97**
Delivery and packing		**£10.00**
Total		**£352.25**

Figure 4: Marked invoice

Accuracy

Dyslexia can make people reverse numbers, lose their place in long numbers and make inaccurate data entries. Because of this, dyslexic employees often lose confidence and indulge in sometimes obsessive over-checking, which is very time-consuming and stressful. Once again, there are some simple things they can do to improve their accuracy.

1   Work slowly and systematically through the data, one chunk at a time. (The chunks may be subsections, lines, columns, single numbers or even parts of numbers.) However pressurized they are, dyslexic people should try not to rush, or their errors will increase: this type of work requires 'making haste slowly'.

2   Check as they go, in small bits, and move on. In effect, they should check figures in the same way that they enter them – one small chunk at a time.

3   Keep their place in the data by ticking off each number, row or column as they complete it.

4   Use associations, whenever they can, to help remember the letter or number chunks they are copying (e.g. GD = 'good'; BR = 'British Rail'; or 28 may be someone's house number/age/birthday, etc.) Also, note familiar bits within numbers to help remember them, such as 007 (James Bond), 501 (Levis); or easy bits like 234, 400 or 88.

5   Try saying the numbers aloud (or whispering them if they are in a busy office). Some people find it much easier to remember numbers if they do this.

6   Learn to trust themselves more. Once they have checked a number carefully, they should try not to dart back and recheck it again and again. This only produces stress, which further hinders accuracy.

7   Place the data they are entering or copying in an easy-to-see position. Simple though it is, this can make a huge difference to their efficiency. They could get a paper-stand with a position-marker to place beside their computer or workbook, where they can see it easily without looking up and down all the time.

8   Finally, dyslexic workers should remember that everyone makes errors copying data, and try not to feel a total failure if they fail to achieve perfection.

Techniques for reading and understanding very complex visual arrays such as graphs and detailed statistical tables are covered in Chapter 14.

Taking phone calls and messages

Dyslexic people often find it very difficult to take phone messages. This basic task involves listening, concentrating and writing all at the same time – and all of these skills can be hampered by dyslexic difficulties. Yet taking phone calls and passing on phone messages form a substantial part of a wide range of different jobs. Many dyslexic people, who have deliberately sought out jobs where they would not be hampered by their difficulties, find themselves in trouble when they find they are expected to deal with phone calls.

> Keme had always had difficulties with reading and writing, and had not done well at school. However, he had strong practical and artistic talents, and was fascinated by photography. He joined a club, and soon became an accomplished photographer. Keme built up an impressive portfolio of his work, which gained him a job as a portrait photographer in a small studio. His portraits were highly praised, but he had problems with other aspects of his new job. Everyone in the studio was expected to do their share of answering phone calls from clients and booking appointments, and Keme was soon in trouble. He found it hard to keep track of what callers were saying at the same time as writing it down. The notes he took were confused and inaccurate: he got names and phone numbers wrong, and muddled the times of appointments. To his colleagues, this seemed like a simple task, and they showed little patience or understanding. After a while, the daily conflict became too much, and Keme left his job. He did not discover until years later that he had dyslexia – and he is at last having training to tackle his difficulties.

Many dyslexic people have suffered the same problems as Keme, and have found their particular skills and talents undermined by their difficulty in dealing with phone calls. However, there are various things they can do to make this task easier

Taking control

The first thing to do is 'take control'. Keeping up with people who talk fast on the phone can be difficult for anyone, but it can seem impossible for dyslexic people, who should learn to stop callers in their tracks if they are going too fast. So the first, simple, rule is to be assertive and ask people to speak more slowly, to repeat things and to spell out names.

Often, dyslexic people are hesitant to do this for fear it will make them seem inefficient, when in fact, it comes across to most people as care and efficiency. (They might think how much more confident they feel when someone takes the trouble to ask them to repeat things in order to ensure that they get their message down fully and correctly.)

There are some people who seem to find it almost impossible to slow down, which can be difficult for a dyslexic person to deal with. In such a situation, it is worth considering whether it might help if they told the caller that they are dyslexic. It is surprising how often this can make someone slow down and try to help.

Dyslexic workers should also get into the habit of reading the message back to the caller to check that they have got it down correctly.

Preparation

For phone messages – as with almost any other task – preparation can make all the difference. Dyslexic people will find things a lot easier if they use their own message format, with clear sections for all the basic information they need to note for most messages, such as date, time, name of caller, caller's position, caller's address, name of recipient, the message and any actions required.

Having a clear, prepared message format with boxed-off blank spaces to write in will make the written message much clearer and more organized, rather than a scrawled, disordered stream of words. It will also serve as a memory aid, to ensure they do not forget to ask for some essential piece of information like the caller's phone number – something that can easily be done with the short-term memory difficulties that dyslexic people suffer.

Writing the message

It will help dyslexic people if they try to use a clear layout when they write down the message itself. They should use headings, bullet points and numbers, and plenty of space. Or they may find it easier to take down the message in the form of a pattern, such as a flow chart with arrows, a spider diagram or a mind map.

They should try *not* to write down any unnecessary words (such as 'the'). It is surprising how much extra time it can take to write all these little words. (If someone said to them, 'Get invoices Accounts Department', they would know exactly what was meant. Yet how much shorter it is than, 'Please would you go to the Accounts Department and get the invoices for me'. (Though admittedly, people might feel more inclined to obey the second order.) Dyslexic people should also get into the habit of using abbreviations whenever they can ('Get invs Ac Dept').

There is more information on note-taking layout and abbreviations in Chapter 13.

DATE:	TIME:
TO	
Name:	Department:
FROM	
Name:	Phone:
Job Title:	FAX:
Address:	E-mail:
MESSAGE	

Figure 5: Example of message format

DATE: 21/06/00	TIME: 10pm
TO	
Name: Mr J Williams	Department: Sales/Mkt
FROM	
Name: Mrs N Gomez	Phone: 0171 777 7777
Job Title: MD	FAX: 0171 777 7771
Address: T & D Insurance Brokers Ltd	E-mail: TD@server.co.uk
22 High Rd	
Woodlington	
Lond	
MESSAGE	

- **INFO WANTED:**
  - Price range laser printers
  - Discs on big orders?
  - Deliv same day?

- **PHONE BACK** - Today - bef 4pm

Figure 6: Layout and abbreviation in phone message

Following instructions

Following oral or written instructions is an ongoing part of any job, but particularly so at the beginning. Just at the time when they are nervously trying to make a good impression and hoping their dyslexic difficulties will not show through, dyslexic new employees are beset by pages of written instructions (frequently not well written) and by a succession of people telling them how to do things. Dyslexic people often feel afraid to appear unable to take in oral instructions or to understand written ones. After asking a few times for explanations, they may give up and hope they will be able to work it out for themselves later.

However, to be able to do a job properly, it is essential for dyslexic employees to get all the instructions fully and clearly, and to understand them. They will be fighting their dyslexic difficulties to be able to do a job efficiently in the best of circumstances. If they do not take control at the initial instruction stage, the job could become overwhelming.

Oral instructions

When taking oral instructions, dyslexic short-term memory difficulties make it hard to retain what is being said. And the problem is compounded by having to take notes at the same time as listening, trying to remember, and keeping the attention focused.

Oral instructions pose many of the same problems as phone calls, but the difficulty is magnified, partly because oral instructions are usually far longer and more detailed than phone calls; and partly because people's ability to do a job properly depends on their getting all the information at the beginning.

The solutions are similar to those for taking phone calls: taking control and asking people to slow down, to repeat things and to explain anything that is not clear. As well as this, in order to ensure that they get all the information, it is not unreasonable for dyslexic employees to ask people to produce written instructions for them as a back-up. (As with requesting repeats in phone calls, this is likely to appear efficient and assertive, rather than incompetent.)

If employers find it difficult to produce clear, written instructions, dyslexic employees might ask them if they would allow them to tape-record the oral instructions. And they should not be afraid to go back and check or ask questions (frequently, if necessary, at first) to ensure that they are doing the job properly. They should also remember that most employers expect – and prefer – staff to do this when they are new in a job, or when they are being given a new task.

Having taken notes of the oral instructions (clearly laid out, with abbreviations, as for phone messages) it will help dyslexic workers immensely if they take the time to write them out in full, in a clear, step-by-step procedure, or in the form of a flow chart. Writing down the procedure will help them to take in the instructions, and will serve as a memory aid for later. It will also give them an overview of all aspects of the task. Once they have written their procedure, they should show it to their boss or supervisor and ask them to check it for any omissions or inaccuracies.

Written instructions

Following written instructions or procedures is also hampered by dyslexia. Frequently, written instructions are not clearly presented and laid out, which makes them even harder to understand.

As mentioned earlier, dyslexic employees should take the time to mark and highlight poorly presented instructions. They should also be assertive and ask their employers to produce clearer instructions – for example with spaces, a large typeface, key words in bold, and clearly numbered sections. It is also very helpful if employers or supervisors produce instructions for dyslexic staff in a less wordy, more concise form, or present instructions more visually, for example in the form of a flow chart.

If the instructions are still hard to follow (and many people have this difficulty, dyslexic or not) then dyslexic workers should muster the confidence to go back and ask for clarification and explanations.

For both written and oral instructions, it will help dyslexic people if they can get someone to work through the job with them the first few times. They can mark any amendments or clarifications on the instruction sheet as they do this. Often, actually doing the job is the quickest and easiest way to learn.

Filing and ordering

Many employers find it hard to understand that so-called simple tasks, such as filing, sorting, or looking things up in indexes or directories, can be very difficult for dyslexic people. Yet these can be among the hardest tasks of all, as they rely heavily on sequencing, word and letter decoding, and short-term memory skills. And it is not just office work that requires ordering and sorting. For example, postmen have to spend part of their day sorting letters by name, address and post code; and many 'practical' jobs involve looking up names and information in phone directories or filing cabinets. Many of the ways to make this type of work easier and more efficient may seem obvious, but it is surprising how few people take the trouble to carry out these obvious strategies.

Dyslexic workers can make simple aids to help them find and keep their place in filing cabinets and directories. For example, many dyslexic people find that it helps if they write out the letters of the alphabet clearly on a large index card, to which they can refer whenever they are filing or searching directories or indexes. The letters should be large, with space between each letter and each row. They can be written in alternating colours, and arranged in small groups of about five letters per line.

a	b	c	d	e
f	g	h	i	j
k	l	m	n	o
p	q	r	s	t
u	v	w	x	y/z

Figure 7: Alphabet card

Dyslexic people will also find filing easier if they take the time to label the contents of the filing cabinets very clearly. They should use prominent and clearly marked coloured dividers between the letters of the alphabet, and perhaps between subgroups within letters if they have a large number of files to search through (e.g. Ab, Ad, Al, Ap, etc., and Ba, Be, Bi, Bl, Bo, Br, etc.).

Simply ensuring that filing cabinets are not too tightly packed can also make a lot of difference.

Looking up names in directories or indexes is harder. On top of the alphabetic sequencing difficulties, there is usually the problem of page after page of closely packed, small print, which is difficult for most people, but particularly difficult for people with dyslexia. It would obviously be too great a task to mark the text in an entire phone directory, but it may help to put index stickers on pages to mark where each letter of the alphabet begins.

For both filing and searching directories, reading the names is very difficult for dyslexic people, many of whom have difficulties with word decoding and sequencing. Many names are long and complex, and many are unfamiliar. In effect, they are facing the sort of task that many dyslexic people dread most - deciphering long sequences of letters that form 'non-words'. As with other tasks, a calm, systematic approach is essential. Similar to reading or spelling, they need to split the names into bits, and to read or search for them chunk by chunk. (For 'Archibald' for example, search first for 'A', then 'Ar', then 'Arch'; then look for the chunk 'ib' and then 'ald').

When reading long names, dyslexic people might use their imagination, and think of their brains as computer scanners, moving methodically and automatically from one syllable to the next, and sounding out each syllable one by one, rather than trying to decode the whole word at once.

If their dyslexia causes them particular difficulty with the sequencing, they could try to see the overall pattern of the name – its length and shape – and see if this helps.

Finally, although filing and directory searching may seem like basic tasks to some (but by no means all) non-dyslexic people, they require a great deal of focused concentration for people who have dyslexia. It will improve their speed and accuracy if they remember to take short breaks in the middle of long filing or searching tasks. If this is not possible, they could try alternating with other types of work that do not require such focused attention.

Project planning

Longer tasks, or projects, can involve a range of different activities and many stages extending over months, or even years. They are likely to involve input from, and interaction with, other people. Keeping control of the different activities, co-ordinating their timing, and keeping everything progressing in the right order to meet the final deadline is difficult at the best of times. For dyslexic employees, it can become a nightmare. They probably have plenty of creative ideas for the project, but getting them in order and putting them into practice may be a different matter altogether.

Just like the overall organization of the whole workload, projects require careful planning, regular monitoring and working through stage by stage.

The importance of planning

The first – and possibly the most important – part of project work is the initial planning stage, before the actual work begins. It is common for people with dyslexia to rush into jobs without planning, often through fear of 'wasting' time, which seems particularly important when dyslexic difficulties are constantly slowing them down. In fact, as mentioned in Chapter 9, the planning actually serves to speed up their progress, by providing them with an overview of the whole job and laying out all the separate activities in order. This frees them to progress steadily through the stages, knowing they have thought everything through and set down a clear plan of action. The resultant feeling of control reduces stress, which would otherwise be an extra hindrance to their progress on top of the dyslexia.

Using the imagination

It may be helpful for dyslexic employees to think of their project plan as if they were using it to make a 'cost quote' for a job they are being paid to do. They could imagine that they will have to quote a price and a completion date for the job based on their project plan (and that the price they quote will be 'all they get', and the completion date they quote will have to be met) even if the job turns out to take a lot more time, effort and resources than they predicted. For, example, if they forget to plan for meetings out of town to liaise with the project workers, they will not be paid for either the time or the fares; they will, in effect, be 'donating' several days of unpaid work and un-refunded fares.

Thinking in this way can help greatly to focus the mind. Project planners need to think of everything, to plan in advance for all the activities involved, and all the time and resources they will need.

It can also help if dyslexic people do the job in their mind as they make the plan. They could imagine themselves actually carrying out the project, and visualize all the stages, requirements and any possible hindrances. Dyslexic people often have very good visual and imaginative skills. They should make use of this strength to envisage the project while they plan it.

Components of the plan

As planners think their way through the project, they will be able to build up a list of its various components. They should note down clearly each activity they think of. They should then think through each particular activity and note down the subtasks that it involves. Dyslexic people will probably find it easier to use a brainstorm spider diagram or mind map to record their initial thoughts. These formats enable them to see the project as a whole on one page, allowing them to see the links between different activities and encouraging creativity. Spider diagrams and mind maps also give the space to cluster related ideas together even if they come to mind out of order, which can happen frequently in dyslexic people.

Starting from the beginning, dyslexic employees should think and imagine their way through the whole project and make a note if it all on their plan. Things to include might be:

- each separate activity (e.g. collection of resources; reading of background material; discussion with other people; data collection;

meetings; travel; planning the project report; and writing the report, section by section)
- subtasks within each activity
- all the equipment and materials that will be needed
- any hindrances they can predict – and actions needed to overcome them
- time schedules and availability of other people involved in the project. (For example, checking whether people will be away at the time their input will be needed, and altering the plan to involve them at an earlier stage. (Many a project has faltered because the person needed 'right now' turns out to be basking in the sun on a distant beach.)

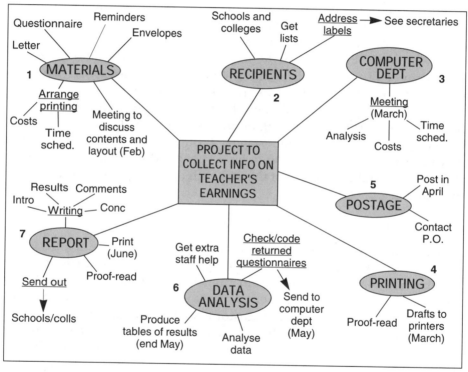

Figure 8: Brainstorm project plan

Writing the plan

Once they feel they have caught and recorded everything on their chart, dyslexic workers should take the time to write it down as a clear, numbered procedure or action plan (see Figure 9). They should remember the importance of layout – it is far easier to work from a plan that looks good and reads well. They may choose to use a flow chart, or a clear, numbered and bulleted list with headings, subheadings, spaces and lines between sections.

Timing

Once the full action plan has been done, it is necessary to estimate how much time each activity will take. Now is the time to turn the attention to each separate bit of the plan, one at a time. Again, dyslexic employees could do each task in their mind, estimate the time it is likely to take and then add a little to allow for the inevitable interruptions and unexpected delays and for the effects of their dyslexia. They should write the time estimates in a different colour beside each activity.

Goals, subgoals and deadlines

Each action on their plan can now serve as a separate subgoal to aim for, with its own deadline. Working through these subgoals should give dyslexic people a sense of progress and achievement, as well as allowing them to monitor their progress.

TEACHERS' EARNINGS	1.
MATERIALS	
- Letter	
- Questionnaire	
- Reminders	
- Envelopes	
Meeting	
- Discuss contents/layout	Early
Arrange printing	Feb
- Costs	
- Time schedules	
RECIPIENTS	
Schools + Colleges	Early
- Get lists	Mar
Address Labels	
- See secretaries	
COMPUTER DEPT	
Meeting	
- Analysis	Early
- Costs	Mar
- Time sched.	

PRINTING	2.
- Drafts to printers	Early Mar
- Proof-read	Mid Mar
POSTING	
- Contact P. O.	Mid Mar
- Post out	Early Apr
DATA ANALYSIS	
- Get extra staff	End Apr
- Check/code	Early May
- Send to Cptr Dept	Mid May
- Analyse data	End May
- Produce tables	End May
REPORT	
Writing	
- Intro	Early Jun
- Results	
- Comments	
- Conclusion	
Print	Mid June
Proof-read	
Send out	End June

Figure 9: Project plan

Of course, they will need to incorporate these project activities and deadlines into their overall work schedule. They should write the 'subdeadline' dates beside each task on their project plan, then copy the tasks on to their overall work action lists (short- and long-term), and enter the deadlines on their calendar and diary. From then on, the routine daily checking of their calendar and action lists, as described in Chapter 10, will keep them reminded of what they should be doing each week and month of the project.

If the project has a stipulated completion date, the breakdown and time estimates will help to show whether or not it will be feasible to meet that date. If not, dyslexic employees should take control now, at the beginning of the project, by showing the project plan to their boss and requesting either extra help or an extended completion date.

Dealing with overload

Many jobs today seem to be becoming increasingly stressful and busy. Overload – and the stress it causes – are particular problems for people with dyslexia. On top of the dyslexic difficulties that slow down performance, the stress becomes an additional hindrance. The important thing is to deal with the problem, and to take control before the overload becomes overwhelming. There are various things they can do.

Acknowledge the problem

First and foremost, the problem has to be acknowledged. So the first thing to do is to accept there is too much work to cope with, tell people about it and start exploring ways to deal with the overload. This may seem obvious, but it is surprising how common it is for people with dyslexia to be hesitant to speak out, for fear that they are at fault - to lack the confidence to admit there is an overload for fear that they will be blamed for it. Wherever the fault lies, the problem will only get worse if they ignore it or try to hide it.

Be assertive and confident

Having acknowledged that an overload exists, dyslexic people should try not to assume automatically that it must be their fault. Their action lists and their recorded appointments and deadlines provide evidence of any overload, and enable them to examine all their work and begin to decide how to deal with it. Even if the problem is partly their fault, having the lists is in itself a sign of efficiency and control, because the lists make them aware of the overload and provide a breakdown of all the work, which is an essential starting point to solving the problem. Dyslexic employees should aim to go through the action lists confidently with their boss or colleagues, and look together for ways to reduce the load. Whenever they can, they should use positive statements, such as 'I will certainly be able to get *this* job done on time, but of course that means I shall have to stop work on *that* job'.

Ask for help

When they talk to their boss and colleagues, dyslexic employees should not be afraid to ask them for help. To begin with, they may need some advice on priority decisions. They may also need some short-term help from other people to enable them to reduce the overload. If the problem is ongoing, they may need to ask for permanent help – or for some of their job to be passed to other people. They could also ask for more efficient tools, such as computer software, to speed up their working. There are many software packages that help greatly to overcome dyslexic difficulties. (There is more information about these in Chapters 12 and 14 on writing and reading, respectively.)

Set priorities

People should look methodically at each job on their action list. They should highlight those with urgent deadlines, and decide whether any other jobs could be shelved or delayed. They should inform their bosses, and anyone else involved, about jobs they plan to delay. If there are still too many urgent jobs, they should take the list to their bosses for decisions on priorities.

Delegate

People with dyslexia often feel unconfident about delegating, because they find it difficult to give clear oral or written instructions. However, if they are in a position to do so, delegating some of their work will be an excellent way to reduce the overload.

Avoid interruptions and distractions

People with dyslexia are likely to be easily distracted – to find their attention wandering again and again from the task in hand. This can cost them a lot of time in a working day, and may well add to the overload. Outside distractions and interruptions make it even harder to keep their attention focused, and they should do what they can to avoid interruptions from people or telephones. For example, close their door; position their desk where it is difficult to get to; not have an empty chair beside their desk; avoid eye contact with people passing their desk; or put up a sign to let people know when they do not want to be disturbed. If possible, they could switch on their telephone answering machine for parts of the day, while they are doing tasks that require particularly heavy concentration.

Chapter 12
General writing skills

Dyslexic people often have an abundance of thoughts and ideas, but they have difficulty expessing these clearly in writing. Most workplace writing needs to be clear, well-structured, and easy to understand. It must also be precise and sharp: no unnecessary verbosity and no long rambling sentences. And it needs to be direct and to the point, covering everything that is required for the task – but without unnecessary frills, and without wandering off the point. Achieving this is not a simple task for anyone. For dyslexic people, this can be one of the greatest obstacles they have to face at work.

Some dyslexic people try to solve the problem by avoiding it. They seek out employment that does not involve writing. But there are very few jobs that do not involve at least some writing. One dyslexic client took a well-paid job as a security guard, only to find that he was expected to produce written reports on any incidents that occurred during his shift. Another had set up his own building firm, but frequently failed to win contracts because of his difficulty with writing clear, coherent job quotations.

To tackle the problem, most dyslexic employees need more than just the advice to 'write clearly and succinctly', and a file of typical formats for business documents. Their underlying – and often deep-seated – difficulty with written expression means that many of them simply do not know how to begin to achieve the clarity and precision of writing that they need to produce at work. And the fear and anxiety that often arise when they sit down to write can sometimes freeze them in their tracks before they start.

First and foremost, most dyslexic people need to learn some basic general techniques for the planning, organizing and structuring of written work. They also need to learn some strategies to tackle the mental barriers that can impede their writing. This chapter aims to 'begin at the beginning' and do just that. It offers guidance to dyslexic and other people on how to develop their general writing skills, and on ways to reduce the stress and anxiety associated with writing. It relates the guidance to workplace writing, with examples relevant to business documents. (The next chapter focuses on the specific formats and requirements of some typical business documents, such as memos, business letters, reports, and workplace note-taking.)

It is particularly important for dyslexic people to develop their basic writing skills. Of all the literacy and organizational difficulties that hamper their performance at work, perhaps the one most likely to stop them in their tracks and block their upward progression is their difficulty with writing.

In most jobs, promotion to higher levels of responsibility means much more writing – more letters and memos, and longer, more complex documents, such as reports and papers for meetings. Usually, these written tasks will need to be done simultaneously, often with conflicting deadlines.

Many dyslexic employees, who may possess all the other requirements for administrative, supervisory or management work, will falter at the prospect of the increased load and complexity of written work that these jobs usually involve.

Often, employers who had perceived talent and promotional potential in dyslexic staff will rapidly revise their opinion when they see their written work. All too often, dyslexic workers' potential is rated by the level of their spelling, punctuation and sentence structure, rather than by their ideas and their brightness.

Shashi is a talented research chemist who used to work for a large pharmaceutical company. She is also dyslexic. In the first few years, her job was mainly laboratory research work, and she did very well. She has a sharp mind, and she was always coming up with useful new ideas and creative proposals. Her talents and initiative were quickly recognized and utilized by her work colleagues and bosses, and she was soon made a team leader.

She managed to cope with this first promotion, as the bulk of her workload was still practical laboratory work. The job gave her more opportunity to display her creative talents. Before long, whenever a new project was undertaken in her department, people came to Shashi for ideas. Whenever a difficult problem arose, Shashi was usually approached – and she usually came up with a workable solution. She became known as the department's problem solver.

The next step up the ladder was to prove more difficult. Shashi's boss decided she was an ideal candidate for higher management, and offered her the job of assistant manager of the department. She knew this would mean much more written work, but with some trepidation she accepted the job. And from that point on, her progress halted.

Shashi had not told her employers that she was dyslexic: it had not seemed relevant to the practical laboratory work she had been initially hired to do. She felt awkward about telling them now, so she just tried as best she could to keep up with the regular load of written work that was a routine part of her new job. But she soon fell behind.

The weekly reports she now had to produce on each of the projects in her department were almost always late, and were viewed as inadequate. She was undoubtedly intelligent, so her bosses assumed that she was simply not bothering to give enough time to the reports. (In fact, she was often up all night writing them.) People still came to Shashi for ideas and solutions, and she was still able to produce them. But now, in her higher position, they expected her to put her ideas into writing. She tried avoidance tactics, asking them to take notes of her ideas, which caused them to see her as difficult and obstructive. She became tired, stressed and frustrated. Her overall work performance declined, even her laboratory work. She began to clash with her boss and colleagues.

Shashi eventually left the job and took on a lower position with another employer, where she firmly resisted any suggestions of promotion. Her excellent talents and her high potential had been lost to both her past and her present employers, simply because of her difficulty with expressing herself in writing.

Shashi is by no means unique. Many highly competent individuals with excellent strategic, creative and problem-solving skills are being wasted in jobs well below their abilities because of their dyslexic difficulties with writing. The cost of their wasted talents is twofold – not only to themselves but also to their prospective employers. Yet with understanding and support from their employers, and with specialist training to tackle their dyslexic difficulties, the full potential of these people could be harnessed and used to their own and their employers' benefit.

The following guidance on general writing skills may help dyslexic employees to make the leap into higher levels of responsibility in their jobs, rather than giving up, as Shashi did.

Planning for written work

Whatever the task – from a short memo to a detailed report – it is essential to plan first. It is especially important for dyslexic people, who have problems with organizing and ordering their ideas, and who often find it difficult to stick to the point.

For many dyslexic people, it is not a matter of lacking ideas, but more a matter of curbing the flow of ideas; of selecting, grouping and linking ideas; and of focusing on the specific requirements of the job in hand. Other dyslexic people have the opposite problem. They feel so daunted at the mere prospect of writing that their minds freeze up and they find it hard to come up with any ideas at all.

For both extremes, good planning can be the answer, because proper planning helps to generate ideas, as well as helping to control them and get them into coherent order. (For those who 'freeze up' at the mere thought of writing, the advice on 'Tackling the block' later in this chapter may help.)

Planning saves time

To many dyslexic people, the task of writing is so arduous in itself that the thought of adding an extra task of planning seems only to increase the load. They are so worried about getting the task completed in time – or about losing track of their ideas – that they leap straight into the writing in the mistaken idea that this will save them time.

This is usually disastrous for anyone, dyslexic or not. Ideas come out in the wrong order – particularly for dyslexic people – and much time-consuming rewriting or cutting and pasting is required. Some good ideas are lost while the writer concentrates on writing down other ideas. The final result is likely to lack coherence and style, and will probably need severe redrafting. All in all, the lack of planning is almost certain to result in more, rather than less time being spent on producing the work.

A separate process

The essential thing is to keep the initial planning separate from the writing proper. Planning and writing are two different processes, involving different skills and attitudes. Trying to do them simultaneously will be to the detriment of both processes. The planning is the creative stage; it requires 'right-brain' activity: seeing the whole picture and allowing ideas and thoughts to flow freely. The subsequent writing stage involves a more logical, sequential approach, concentrating on sentence structure, punctuation and spelling, and using the left hemisphere of the brain.

Aspects of planning

Effective planning involves several different aspects.

1 Clarifying the aim and requirements of the task.
2 Brainstorming for ideas.

3   Clustering and grouping ideas.
4   Ordering and linking ideas.
5   Planning the introduction and conclusion.

The aim and requirements of the writing task

However creative or free-flowing the planning stage is, it still needs to focus on the particular aims and requirements of the task in hand. This is particularly important for workplace writing, which usually needs to be clear, succinct and to the point. This is not easy for dyslexic people, whose thoughts tend to wander off the point. On top of this, their short-term memory difficulties can make them forget the point altogether and lose track of the specific aims and requirements of the task. They are also likely to find it hard to keep their concentration focused, which can make them lose the thread.

For these reasons, the planning process should begin with some careful thought about exactly what the written communication requires. This means not just the subject matter, but also the aim or purpose of the writing (its desired outcome) and its audience. Each of these will affect what needs to be covered in the plan. So the writer needs to think clearly, at the very beginning, about the full requirements of a piece of writing, and to sketch out an initial 'skeleton' plan with a heading or section for each requirement or key point.

Even a brief memo always has its own subject, aim and purpose. For example, it may need to obtain or to provide information on a particular subject, or to put forward a particular opinion. For a memo seeking information and guidance about dyslexic staff employed in a company, the skeleton plan would need to start with the following essential headings:

*   introduction
*   reasons for requesting information
*   information required
*   guidance required
*   when information required by
*   conclusion.

Each of these main headings needs to be written on the skeleton plan at the outset - to remind the dyslexic worker of the key points to be covered and to provide a framework for the subsequent brainstorming for ideas.

For a report, there are likely to be clear guidelines as to the main headings required for the skeleton plan. For example, in a problem-solving report, the essential main sections on the plan would be the introduction, the problem, the possible solutions, the assessment of the solutions and the conclusion.

A long report may need several plans: one 'overview' plan for the whole report; and a series of more detailed 'sub-plans' for each section of the report. (There is more information on report writing in the next chapter.)

Brainstorming

The next stage is the creative one – generating the detailed ideas for the written piece. Dyslexic people often have an abundance of ideas, and the skeleton plan will help them keep these ideas on the point. The headings will also remind them of all the areas in which they need to generate ideas, and ensure that they do not forget any of the basic requirements.

There are various different formats for brainstorming. These include mind-maps, spider diagrams, flow charts,and even linear 'box plans' with separate ruled-off sections for each main heading and bullet points for the subheadings. People should choose the format they feel easiest with, or that best suits the task in hand. However, the mind-map or spider diagram are particularly effective for brainstorming. They allow the planner to see the whole picture in one go, and they show the links and interrelationships between the sections. And their visual, rather than linear, layout appeals to most dyslexic people.

Whatever format is chosen, with the skeleton plan as a basis to steer the planner in the right direction, this is the time simply to let go and let the ideas flow – as they arise. As the ideas crop up, they can be briefly noted on the appropriate section, box, or 'prong' of the plan. It is sensible to leave plenty of space around each separate heading, to allow room to cluster related ideas together.

Of course, completely new ideas may arise that require new sections or prongs; the skeleton plan was only an initial framework of essential ingredients. Any new ideas must, of course, be relevant to the subject. To ensure this, all plans need a clear and full title or heading to remind the planner of the subject.

For those who find it difficult to generate ideas, it might be helpful to use the imagination to give the mind a nudge. For example, for the memo requesting information and guidance about dyslexic staff, planners might try to imagine and visualize the dyslexic employees they are enquiring about. They could think of dyslexic staff in different types of work, picture them doing their jobs and wonder what sorts of people they are and what difficulties they might encounter. These thoughts will probably give rise to questions, and help the planner to think of specific details they would like to request in their memo.

During the brainstorming, the skeleton plan for the memo might develop as shown below.

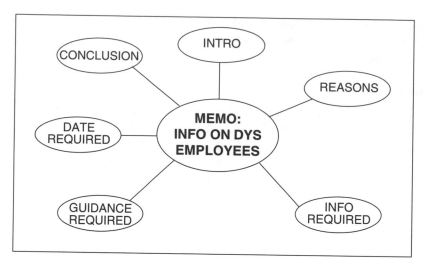

Figure 10: Skeleton plan for memo

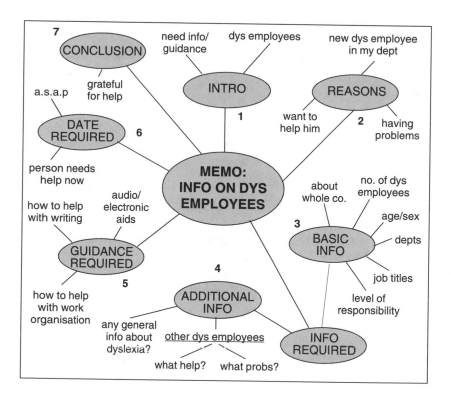

Figure 11: Full plan after brainstorming

Information can sometimes become very crushed and confused on a brainstorm plan, which can make it hard to read. Once the brainstorm is done, dyslexic workers will find it easier to read if they use different coloured highlighters to colour each prong, and to encircle the information linked to that prong. In fact, anything done to improve or enliven the presentation of the plan, such as highlights, colours, circles, boxes, and underlines or capitals for headings and subheadings, will make it easier for dyslexic people to work from.

The next thing to do is to check that everything on the plan is relevant to the subject, and to delete anything that is not. (Dyslexic people often find stray, unrelated ideas creeping into their plans.) Finally, they should then check to make sure that there is something on the plan for each aspect of the subject.

Of course, some writing tasks are more open-ended, without clear guidelines for main topics (for example, a proposal paper for ideas for new work projects). In this case, the spider diagram or mind map is a good medium to let the mind run free on the subject, just catching whatever ideas occur and noting them on the plan.

Clustering

Another thing that dyslexic people find difficult is organizing their thoughts into clusters of related ideas as they write. The work of dyslexic employees is often criticized for wandering backwards and forwards between topics without any clear, coherent thread.

Because the spider diagram allows the planner to see the whole picture, it is an ideal format to encourage clustering. The ideas may come out in their own disordered way, but they can be written down next to similar ideas on the plan, automatically forming a set of separate clusters.

Ordering and linking

The next task is to get the clusters into a logical order, and to link them together to form a logical and coherent progression of ideas throughout the memo, letter or report. Obviously, the introduction comes first and the conclusion last, but the bits in the middle can become muddled. The planner needs to look at all the clusters, decide on the most logical order to present them, and then clearly number them on the plan.

With the ideas already grouped into sections, putting them in order should not be as difficult as it may at first seem to many dyslexic writers. Certain sections will fall into a clear sequence (for example, 'basic information' will naturally come before 'additional information' in the above memo plan). And there will be natural links between some sections. (For example, the section on 'additional information' ended with a question about what help dyslexic staff were getting. This leads naturally into the section on 'guidance', which asks how to help a particular dyslexic staff member.)

First and last impressions

It is through the introduction and conclusion that the powerful first and last impressions are conveyed. Their effect on the readers is strong, and so dyslexic people would be well advised to plan the contents of these sections particularly carefully. They should also check these sections in detail for any errors in spelling, punctuation or sentence structure.

The introduction

As the first impression, the introduction should – if at all possible – aim to capture the readers' interest. Of course, this is not always possible in routine business letters or memos, or in reports on dull subjects, but the introduction should at least provide a 'taster' by outlining the main theme and points that the written piece will cover. An introduction might include:

- a reference to the main subject and theme
- a brief statement of the aim or purpose of the piece
- a succinct summary of what is to be covered
- a suggestion of how the ideas will be developed.

The conclusion

The conclusion should round off the subject and form the final link in the chain.

- It might refer back to the beginning and resummarize the key points.
- It should summarize any final arguments, opinions or decisions.
- It might look ahead to future possibilities and make recommendations.

Whatever form the conclusion takes, it *must* follow logically from the rest of the written piece.

The effect of planning

As well as collecting thoughts and getting them into order, having a plan helps to relieve two major impediments that plague many dyslexic people: the anxiety and stress they feel when they start to write, about not knowing what to say and where to begin; and the feelings of confusion and lack of control that this inevitably causes.

The completion of the plan should make writers feel much more relaxed and in control. They have planned everything they want to include in the written piece; and they have arranged it into sections and put it in order. This should be a huge load off their mind. They do not have to worry about what to include, or whether it is in the right place, at the same time as trying to write. Theoretically, it should be a relatively straightforward matter of proceeding through each section of the plan, one at a time, and putting the ideas into words.

However, for people with dyslexia, this is by no means a simple matter. Having the plan undoubtedly relieves them of a large part of the problem, but converting it into sentences poses further difficulties. The planning was a crucial beginning – and having done it will make the task of writing easier and less daunting – but it is still only a beginning.

Tackling the block

The plan may make the writer feel more in control, but dyslexic people will still suffer from doubts and uncertainties. Perhaps the first thing to tackle, when they sit down to write from the plan, is the mental aspect — the lack of confidence, the negative expectations, the fears and the doubts (and sometimes the feelings of sheer panic or revulsion) at the prospect of starting to write.

These negative states are often revealed in the body language of dyslexic people. Their muscles become tense, their shoulders hunch up, and their facial expressions reflect hopelessness and distaste. With all these negative emotions on top of their dyslexic difficulties, the flow of writing can freeze up completely.

This fear of writing, and the freezing up in front of the computer, are at their worst under conditions of stress and pressure – conditions that commonly occur in a busy, working environment, where dyslexic employees may be faced with tight deadlines for written reports or growing piles of correspondence to be dealt with.

Many people who are not dyslexic also suffer negative feelings when faced with a complex writing task. But few of them understand the full extent and the full effect of these negative emotions on dyslexic people, who have very real underlying problems with basic writing skills.

It is important that dyslexic people acknowledge the damage that their state of mind can do to their writing, and that they work to tackle their fears and doubts along with their underlying writing difficulties. Many dyslexic people work with great determination and effort to build up their writing skills, yet they still freeze up when they start to write, and produce clumsy sentences with errors. They may have worked to acquire the underlying skills, but their minds will not believe it.

It can be hard to tackle these mental blocks. The negative attitudes are likely to be deeply ingrained after many years of failure, and they do not drop away easily. But they must be addressed, and there are a number of things that dyslexic people can do to help reduce them.

Stress reduction

As mentioned earlier, stress is one of the worst conditions for mental performance. Relaxation exercises can help immensely to reduce stress and calm fears, which will help to increase clarity of mind and release the writing flow. Simply taking deep breaths before writing, and loosening up tense muscles and body posture, can help a lot. It is also advisable to set up a routine of regular, daily relaxation exercises, which will steadily reduce the general feelings of stress and anxiety over time. (There is more on relaxation and stress reduction in Chapter 16.)

Levels of stress can also be significantly increased by trying too hard. Paradoxically, if dyslexic workers stop trying and just write down whatever comes out (while following their plan, of course), they often find that the style and quality of their writing improves.

'Talk and copy'

Many dyslexic people are adequate, and often extremely competent, at oral expression. But everything snarls up when they try to put their thoughts into written form. Those who are orally competent can find it especially difficult to get understanding and support from their employers, who perceive their intelligence in their oral expression, and tend to assume they are just being 'lazy' about writing things down. However, these people can take advantage of their oral skills by putting them to work to help their writing.

Some dyslexic employees find that it helps greatly if they dictate from their plan into a tape recorder or dictaphone, and then type or copy from the tape. Others find that simply speaking each phrase or sentence aloud (or under their breath) to themselves, and then immediately copying what they have said, can greatly improve the quality and flow of their writing.

Using the imagination

As in other areas, dyslexic people can use their often active imaginations to help with their writing flow. Dyslexic people tend to forget that writing is not just 'words on a page', but a real communication between individuals. It can help if they deliberately think of their writing as a 'living communication' and use their imagination to picture themselves talking directly to the recipients of their writing. Instead of just sitting down and typing their way through a pile of business letters, they could imagine themselves going to the offices of the people they are writing to and telling them face to face what they want to say. For a report or a meeting paper, they could try to imagine themselves giving a talk or a lecture, and feel the words flowing as they speak directly to their audience.

One particular dyslexic employee has succeeded in markedly improving her writing flow by sticking a large poster of a friendly-looking person on the wall in front of her desk and imagining that she is speaking to the person in the poster whenever she writes.

Dyslexic people can also use their imagination in less specific ways to improve their writing. One person imagines, as he starts to write, that his mind is a huge dam; he then visualizes the floodgates opening and letting the words pour out.

Using the imagination, or speech, to encourage the flow of writing may not produce error-free work, but at least it can help to get the words flowing. The writer can then check back to look for errors, almost like doing the task as two separate people: first as the 'writer', then as the 'editor'.

Co-operation from co-workers

The behaviour and attitude of the bosses and work colleagues of dyslexic employees can be an extra factor that adds to their feelings of stress and anxiety, and that further hampers their writing performance. Most dyslexics find it almost impossible to write while being watched or pressurised – and the anxious, hovering boss can be a severe impediment to the dyslexic employee's writing progress. Colleagues who interrupt or create distractions can also disrupt the focus and concentration. Dyslexic employees should consider explaining this to their bosses and colleagues, and asking them to help by avoiding hovering or interrupting while they are writing.

The writing process

As mentioned above, even with a good, well-presented plan, the process of writing is by no means 'plain sailing' for dyslexic employees. And even using the above techniques to help the words flow, there will still be problems with basic spelling, punctuation and grammar, and with sentence structure and writing style. These very basic skills are not covered in this book. There are many books already published on these, and many specialist groups and tutors who can help dyslexic people acquire these skills. The following pages offer some guidelines on how to improve the overall structure and coherence of written work.

Working in stages

The familiar refrain of working in stages, one step at a time, and taking breaks in between, applies to writing as much as to any other task. The plan itself should provide a clear series of separate sections and subsections. Each one should be written out like a separate task, with a break before the next stage if the concentration is flagging. In the same step-by-step way, a pile of correspondence can be tackled a letter at a time, with breaks between letters. In a busy job where breaks are not easy to take, dyslexic employees should try alternating their writing with other, less demanding, tasks.

Psychologically, it will be easier for the dyslexic worker to face writing a small section, or a single letter or memo, than to face a whole report or a large heap of letters. The breaks between stages allow writers to refresh their concentration. And, of course, it is very good for motivation, and for getting a sense of progress, to tick off each stage on a plan one by one, or see a pile of letters steadily reducing in size.

The logical thread: announcing and linking ideas in written work

A good piece of writing will have a clear progression of ideas - a logical train of thought running through it from beginning to end. The planning will have helped dyslexic writers to organize their ideas into a clear train of thought.

However, it is no use if the writer knows the train of thought but fails to pass it on to the readers. This will leave readers with the task of constantly having to work out for themselves, as they read, what each new section or paragraph is about, and how it relates to other bits of the document. They will be confused by sudden, unannounced changes of subject or direction, and will keep having to go back to check the logic. They will probably not persist to the end of the document.

To keep them reading – and understanding – readers need to be kept fully informed, throughout the document, about what is coming up, and about how it relates to what went before. To achieve this, the writer needs to include '**announcements**' and '**logical links**' whenever there is a change of subject or direction in the writing. These act like a 'thread' running through the document, weaving the separate sections and paragraphs together to form a continuous flow of thought and a coherent whole.

Announcements

Just as every document needs a general introductory section or paragraph that tells readers what the document is about, so each change of subject within a document needs its own brief introduction.

Each subsection of a document needs an introductory sentence or paragraph that 'sets the scene' for the readers – in effect 'announcing' to them the main subject of the forthcoming section. And each paragraph needs a topic sentence at the beginning, which announces the theme of the paragraph. Some examples are given below.

Announcement of a main section

"This section looks at the advantages of setting up the new computer system. It covers not only the long-term cost/benefits, but also the enhanced speed and efficiency that the new system will bring to all departments. It also looks at other benefits, such as the relative ease of learning the new system."

Announcement of a subsection

"One of the main advantages of the new computer system is its greater efficiency, which will speed up work throughout the company."

Announcement ('topic sentence') of a paragraph

"Efficiency will also be enhanced by the system's excellent database."

Announcements like these are essential to keep the readers aware of each change of subject. Without them, readers are left floundering around trying to work out what each subject is. (It is as if someone keeps suddenly changing the subject in a conversation without announcing the fact – leaving the listener always one step behind, struggling to make sense of the flow of changing information.) In contrast, with frequent clear announcements, readers will be able to flow effortlessly and quickly through a piece of writing.

Linking

As well as announcements, written documents also need linking words or phrases. These tell the readers how a section, paragraph or sentence is logically related to the one before. These links are usually placed at the beginning (or close to the beginning) of the 'announcement' to the section or paragraph, or at the beginning of a sentence. The links take the form of single words or short phrases that inform the readers of the logic or direction of the written ideas.

For example, a link may inform the readers that the next bit of writing will be in contrast to the previous one; or that it will be more of the same; or that it will be a consequence of the previous thing. Or it may indicate the time relationship (e.g. subsequently...) or the content (e.g. fortunately...). The following sentences all contain examples of linking words or phrases.

- *In addition* to the general induction procedures, all new staff members must be shown a copy of the office safety regulations.
- New staff members should *also* be given copies of their job descriptions to sign.
- *In contrast*, the old system was difficult to learn and often broke down.
- *However*, the system could be made easier to learn if the instruction manuals are rewritten.
- *As a result* of the late payments of invoices, we shall have to consider reviewing our accounting procedures.
- *Because* of this, we have seriously overspent our budget.
- *Previously*, we had always kept within budget by cutting back on new projects.

It may help dyslexic people to think of these linking words and phrases as signposts on a road. Omitting announcements and links is like sending readers blindly down unsignposted roads, with no idea of what place they are heading for, or in what direction they are travelling, and having to find out for themselves as they go. In these circumstances, many travellers will quickly abandon the journey – as readers will abandon the document.

Thinking of announcements and links

Often, dyslexic writers are having to put so much thought and attention into simply getting the words out, spelling them correctly and forming them into sentences, that they forget about the announcements and links, or find it hard to do this at the same time as writing. The following guidelines may be helpful.

1 **Use the plan.** The plan itself contains sections and subsections. Each

of these needs its own announcement. It can help dyslexic writers to think of announcements, if they go back to the plan and jot down (on the plan) a brief introductory sentence to announce each section on the plan. (These could be written in a different colour, to remind the writer to type them first.)

2 **Subheadings.** In a formal document like a report, the announcements may be taken care of by the use of headings and subheadings, which do the job of announcing what is coming next. In a piece of writing that does not include subheadings, it may help dyslexic people if they think what subheadings might be inserted (i.e. what is the main point or core topic of the section) and then write a short introductory sentence incorporating that.

3 **Become familiar with linking words/phrases.** It will help dyslexic people if they become familiar with the common linking words and phrases. The following list gives a number of common ones, divided up into logical categories. Dyslexic workers could take a copy of the list and keep it on their desk or beside their computer. When checking a piece of writing, they should think about how each section or paragraph relates logically to the one before. (Is it giving more of the same information? Is it giving contrasting information? Is it a consequence of what went before?) They could then choose an appropriate word or phrase from the list below, and insert it at the beginning of the relevant section or paragraph.

Examples of linking words and phrases

- **To indicate addition (more on the same subject):** 'In addition...'; 'also...'; 'likewise...'; 'furthermore...'; 'secondly...'; 'similarly...'
- **To indicate contrast:** 'In contrast...'; 'however...'; 'on the other hand'; 'yet...'; 'in spite of...'; 'neverthless...'
- **To indicate cause or effect:** 'As a result of...'; 'because of...'; 'therefore...'; 'consequently...'; 'in order to...';.
- **To indicate time relationships:** 'subsequently...'; 'previously...'; 'then...'; 'whenever...'; 'next...'; 'frequently...'.
- **Illustrations:** 'for example...'; 'for instance...'.
- **To indicate content:** 'fortunately...'; 'unfortunately...'; 'surprisingly...'; 'strangely...'; 'primarily...'.

Finally, although the main purpose of links and announcements is to help readers follow the thread, thinking of them will also help dyslexic writers to stick to the thread. It will make them aware, for example, if they are skipping back and forth between similar and contrasting information instead of clustering it all together in two main groups. And it will reveal when a particular subject has got out of order, or is not relevant to the document.

Ordering

The sequencing difficulties of dyslexic people can make it hard for them to get their thoughts in the correct order. This is why the numbering of sections in the plan is important. However, there must also be a logical order *within* sections and *within* paragraphs. Within a paragraph or section, the information needs to be arranged in a hierarchy such as that shown below:

- introductory statement announcing the theme of the paragraph or section
- elaboration or expansion
- examples or illustrations
- arguments or evaluations
- conclusions.

Of course, not all of these will be appropriate to every paragraph or section, but they need to appear in that order. Dyslexic people may find it useful to write the above hierarchy on a card and keep it for reference when organizing information within paragraphs or sections.

Keeping it simple

It may seem surprising that many dyslexic people have a tendency to use far too many long words and sentences in their writing. Paradoxically, this can be caused by their lack of confidence in their writing skills, and embarrassment at their relatively sparse vocabulary. This can make them feel they have to strive to use long words and complicated sentences to disguise their weaknesses. In other cases, it is because the words and sentences seem to stream out in a confused muddle, producing long and often incoherent sentences.

In fact, short words and sentences are usually very powerful. They can achieve a clarity and precision that is exactly what is needed in most work reports and business letters. Dyslexic employees should bear this in mind. They should aim to write short, clear sentences whenever possible, and not to use a long word when a short one will do. They should remember that a sentence is supposed to contain only one unit of thought (one idea or one piece of information). They should also get into the habit of using the shorter, active tense, instead of the passive tense. For example, '*The Accounts Department will send you the information you need*', instead of '*The information you require will be forwarded to you by the Accounts Department*'. They should also try to avoid unnecessary 'frills'. One or two examples or illustrations are usually enough, there is no need for five or six.

Of course, verbose and jargon-filled reports and business letters are written every day by non-dyslexic people. They are difficult to read and understand. More importantly, they fail to achieve their main purpose – of communicating ideas clearly and coherently to their readers. Dyslexic employees might find it good practice to look at such documents with a critical eye, and see if they can make the wordy sentences shorter and clearer. Some examples are given below. (The list provides far more examples than you were advised to give earlier in this section. This is because dyslexic readers may wish to use the examples below as a short exercise, to see if they can think of shorter ways to express the wordy sentences at the beginning of each example.)

- *'The remuneration paid to managers in top positions exceeds by a very considerable amount the salaries that are paid to people in non-managerial types of work'* could be shortened to *'The pay of top managers is far higher than that of people in non-managerial work'*.

- *'We are now in a position to make you an offer of employment on a full-time basis'* could become *'We can offer you a full-time job'*.

- *'There is a considerable probability that this plan will not produce a successful outcome'* could become *'This plan will probably not succeed'*.

- *'She was of the opinion that there was no necessity for the engaging of part-time workers'* could become *'She thought they would not need part-time workers'*.

- *'They expended a great deal of effort in their attempt to provide a solution to the problem'* could become *'They worked hard to solve the problem'*.

- *'Please ensure that a programme is provided to every person'* could become *'Please give everyone a programme'*.

- *'In the event of your being ill, I would require you to inform me'* could become *'Please tell me if you are ill'*.

- *'Under no circumstances whatever should you attempt to proceed to the top of this mountain without company'* could become *'Never climb this mountain alone'*.

Checking

Because of their underlying difficulties in basic writing skills, it is important that dyslexic people allocate some time at the end of their writing to go back over their work and check it for spelling and punctuation errors, and for clarity and coherence. Their reading difficulties, of course, may make it hard for them to spot any errors, and we all tend to 'see' what we expect. It is best to check the words one bit at a time, as any sequencing errors will probably not be noticed by looking at the whole word.

This is a stage when it can be very useful for dyslexic staff to enlist the help of their work colleagues. If colleagues are made aware of the dyslexic person's difficulties, they may be willing to help by checking their final draft for errors.

It can also help if dyslexic people read their work aloud to themselves to see if it 'sounds' clear and coherent. Or they can use text-to-voice computer software to allow them to listen and read at the same time.

Writing aids

There is a wide and growing range of computer software and audio equipment that is making life more and more easy for dyslexic people. Dyslexic employees should make full use of this equipment at work. They need to become aware of what is available, and to ask their employers to provide equipment that can help them with their work.

Word-processing software

First and foremost, dyslexic employees should take advantage of the most user-friendly software packages they can find. Then they should ask for proper training on how to use it. On any training courses, they should inform the trainers about their dyslexia and ask for extra time, attention and guidance. They should also look for the best-presented instruction manuals they can find. (The *Teach Yourself Visually* instruction books in the 3-D Visual Series by IDG Books are especially effective for dyslexic people.)

Spellcheckers

The spellcheckers on all modern word-processing software have proved a godsend to dyslexic people. The important thing is to use the spellchecker properly and learn from it. Many people simply click the corrected words rapidly without stopping to take note of their errors. This may save time in the short term, but it means they will remain dependent on the spellchecker. The number of errors they make will not decrease, and they will continue to spend valuable time being alerted to the same spelling errors over and over again.

For this reason it is recommended that, whenever they can, dyslexic workers should take at least a little time to notice the types of errors they make. They should pinpoint each error and notice, for example, whether it occurs in a common word bit (such as '-ity' or '-tious'). If it does, they should write down and become familiar with that word bit, which will crop up in a range of different words.

They should also practise a few simple memory techniques, such as pronouncing the word aloud as it is spelt, visualizing the word, typing it out a few times and noticing the different syllables it contains. They could also think of simple memory tricks to help remember the spellings (for example, 'be<u>lie</u>ve a <u>lie</u> or 'meet your fri/end at <u>Fri</u>day's <u>end</u>).

For difficult words that crop up frequently in their work, they could also keep a notebook by the computer, and write the words in the book to refer to later.

All of this may seem time consuming, and there will certainly not always be time to do it in a busy job. But if it is done whenever possible, it will mean that, slowly but surely, spellings are learned, and less and less valuable time is spent with the spellchecker.

It is advisable to find a spellchecker that also alerts the writer to homophones (words that sound the same but are spelt differently, such as 'made' and 'maid' or 'council' and 'counsel'). The use of the wrong homophone escapes many spellcheckers.

Voice dictation systems

There are some very good voice dictation systems on the market. These can be a huge help to dyslexic people, enabling them to speak their thoughts directly on to the computer screen. The voice dictation systems can take some time to be 'trained' to recognize the individual's voice and accent, but most dyslexics find that the results are well worth the effort.

Text-to-speech software

This software can be a great help to dyslexic writers. It reads text aloud from the computer screen, enabling dyslexic people to hear what they have written and to detect poor writing style or lack of clarity. For example, *Text Help*, by Lorien Systems, will read aloud word by word, sentence by sentence, or whole highlighted sections of text. It runs in tandem with other software programmes, and includes a range of other features, including a spellchecker and a homophone checker.

Creative software

There are also software packages that help people to brainstorm for ideas and to get their ideas clustered and organized. They provide visual formats such as spider diagrams, flow charts and family trees in which people can group and manipulate ideas while planning for a written piece. One of these, which many dyslexic people have found helpful, is called *Inspiration*.

Audio tapes and dictaphones

As mentioned previously, dyslexic employees often find that talking into a tape recorder or dictaphone, and then typing from their own dictation, helps their writing. Tape recorders are also useful as an alternative to taking written notes of meetings, discussions and oral instructions. This is particularly helpful to dyslexic people, many of whom find note-taking at speed very difficult to do.

* * * * * *

The range and sophistication of equipment that can help with writing is growing every day. This section has given only a brief overview of some of the equipment that is currently available. Chapter 21 includes information on organizations and individuals that can be contacted to offer advice and information on such equipment.

Chapter 13
Some specific work documents

Most business documents have distinct set formats. This can be very helpful to dyslexic employees. The laid-down structure and formats of business documents provide a clear 'skeleton' framework into which they can slot their ideas. They should keep a file of typical formats to refer to whenever they need it.

This chapter provides some guidelines on the formats, requirements and typical contents of several different business documents. It also includes some basic advice and guidelines on note-taking, which can be particularly difficult for dyslexic staff.

However, in addition to learning the standard formats of business documents, it will help dyslexic employees if they take the time at the beginning of a new job to become familiar with the specific types of documents that are commonly used in that particular job. This may take a little extra time at the beginning, but it will save a lot of time in the long run. When starting a new job, dyslexic employees should ask for examples of past memos, letters, reports and other documents that they will be expected to write. As well as the formats, this will also give them an idea of the writing style favoured by their employers; and they will be able to find typical words and expressions, and use these in their own work.

Having a set of sample documents will also show the employer's 'house style'. (Each company or organization has its own individual house style for the layout and writing of their documents.)

It will also save time if dyslexic employees keep some samples of their own work documents. Most jobs involve a fair amount of repetitious work – the routine production of written documents on the same recurring subjects. For example, a job might require the frequent writing of memos or letters providing the same or similar information to different people. Or it may involve the regular production of reports or updates on recurring subjects. As they progress in the job, dyslexic employees should keep a file of typical examples of their writing on various subjects. This will save them from having to think up words and expressions over and over again for each new piece of writing. If they keep a set of these examples in a separate file in their computer, they will be able to save time by simply cutting and pasting common sentences or paragraphs instead of typing them again and again.

The rest of this chapter provides some basic information and guidelines on some typical work documents.

Memos

Ideally, memos should be informal, and they should be very brief and concise. On the surface of it, this might seem to be relatively simple compared with other, longer writing tasks. In reality, it is often easier to write at length than to condense the information into the short memo form. Dyslexic people often find it hard to select and pare down information. They can have trouble focusing on the core points and discarding the 'frills'. One busy dyslexic manager used to sum up his feelings with a routine introduction to many of his memos and letters: 'I am sorry this letter is so long. I did not have the time to write a short one.'

Planning the memo

People tend to think that a memo is too short to need planning. But this can be a mistake. Although short, memos still need a clear structure, with an introduction, a conclusion and separate paragraphs. A plan will help dyslexic workers to structure their memo and to cluster and order the contents.

Furthermore, if people simply start writing, without thinking beforehand, they are likely to write too much. They need to take a little time to think first of what are the central points they want to communicate (what information they are seeking or providing; what suggestions they want to put forward, etc.). The plan enables them to focus on the key points. As the plan progresses, the key points should stand out, and any unnecessary frills can be crossed out. (See Chapter 12 for more details on memo writing.)

The memo format

The style and format of a memo will vary from company to company. Some firms will have preprinted memo forms. Others will have a set house style for memos and other documents.

All memos require:

- the date
- the name of the writer
- the name of the recipient

A typical memo format is as follows.

MEMORANDUM	
	Date:
To:	
From:	
Subject of memo	

The contents of the memo

The memo itself should be as brief and clear as possible. It should stick to the point, covering everything that is necessary, but nothing that is irrelevant.

Like any written work, the content of a memo should have a coherent, logical progression. It should have an introduction and a conclusion, and there should be appropriate announcements and link words or phrases to indicate clearly the direction of the argument.

The writing should be concise, with no unnecessary padding, no repetitions and no long words or expressions where short ones will do.

Unlike a letter, a memo does not begin with 'Dear...' or end with 'Yours sincerely'.

The heading

Although a heading is not essential, it provides a clear and immediate statement of the subject. It also allows a shorter introduction to the memo (e.g.: 'I have a query on the above subject').

The introduction

The introduction should state briefly:

1. the subject of the memo (if it is not covered in the heading);
2. the reason for writing the memo (e.g.: 'In response to your telephone request...').

The main body of the memo

The middle section of the memo should present all the relevant information in a logical order. It might include, for example:

* a request for information
* reasons for the request
* date by which the information is required.

The conclusion

The concluding paragraph should cover such things as:

* the outcome of the matter (e.g. when any information requested will be ready)
* any overall conclusions or recommendations.

Business letters

The 'rules' for writing business letters are very similar to those for writing memos. Although they are generally longer than memos, they also need to be as clear and concise as possible; and they also need a clear structure with the usual introduction and conclusion, separate paragraphs for each change of subject, and announcements and links to provide a clear, logical progression of ideas. (Most of the general guidelines given in Chapter 12 will apply to the writing of business letters.)

The basic components of a business letter are:

* the date
* the writer's reference number (not essential, but it will help with filing)
* the company's address and phone number; and the fax number and e-mail address if relevant (all these are usually incorporated in the company letterhead)
* the recipient's address
* a heading to the letter (not essential, but it helps make the subject clear to the reader).

A typical layout for a business letter is shown below.

LETTERHEAD

Company Address

Phone Number

Our reference:
Your reference:
21 June 2000

Mr W B Davis
Address.........
....
....
....

Title of letter

Dear Mr Davis,

If there is not a company letterhead, the writer's address and phone number would appear at the top right, above the reference numbers.

Reports

Reports are usually long and complex. Writing them can be very daunting to dyslexic employees. However, with a good plan, a report can be tackled one section at a time, which will make it much more manageable.

Reports have very clear formal structures, which provide a good framework to work within. All reports need separate sections for a summary, an introduction, the main body of the report (which is usually made up of several sections) and a conclusion. They may also require a background section, a discussion section and a section for recommendations. It is essential that they have a very clear logical thread, beginning in the introduction and weaving through each section of the report and on to the conclusion.

The precise format of each report depends on its particular aims and purpose. For example, the purpose of a report may be simply to provide information; or it may aim to persuade or to make recommendations; or to assess different proposals or options.

The following examples give brief outlines of the formats of several different types of report.

Informative report

Title page

Contents page

Summary

Introduction

Presentation of information

(with subsections for each different type of information)

Conclusion

Bibliography/references

Appendices

Problem-solving report

Title page

Contents page

Summary

Introduction

The problem(s)

Possible solution(s)

Assessment of solution(s)

Discussion

Conclusion

Recommendations

Bibliography/references

Appendices

Feasibility report

Title page

Contents page

Summary

Introduction

Current position

Proposal(s)

Evidence in favour of proposal(s)

Evidence against proposal(s)

Discussion

Conclusion

Recommendations

Bibliography/references

Appendices

Research report

Title page

Contents page

Summary

Introduction

Methodology

Results

Discussion

Conclusion

Recommendations

Bibliography/references

Appendices

Planning the report

For a lengthy, detailed document like a report, it is essential to get a clear overview of the whole thing at the outset. As stated in Chapter 12, mind-maps and spider charts are very effective for getting an overview. The initial skeleton plan should include a separate heading or prong for each subsection of the report, as listed in the examples above.

The planning stage will allow dyslexic employees to collect together all their information and ideas, and to allocate them to the correct section of the plan. A series of subplans can then be made for each separate section of the report. (See details on planning written work in Chapter 12.)

Writing the report

Once the plan has been done, dyslexic people should narrow down their focus to deal with one section at a time, and treat each section as a separate writing task. Thinking of just one section at a time will be a lot less stressful than trying to tackle the whole report in one go. As with all types of business writing, the writing style should be as simple, clear and jargon-free as possible. (See Chapter 12.)

The following guidelines give more details of the contents of reports.

Basic report structure and contents

Title page

- clear, concise title
- author(s)
- date.

Contents page

- list of main sections and subsections with page numbers
- list of appendices.

Summary

- brief summary of the whole report, covering all main points

Introduction

- background to the report (what 'went before it')
- reasons for writing the report
- purpose, aims and objectives
- scope of the report.

(The above might become separate headed sub-sections in a long report.)

Main body of the report

Within the main body of the report, there will usually be several separate sections. These will vary according to the type of report (as in the examples of different report formats above.)

The main body of the report may include the following.

'Descriptive' sections

These sections will provide information about what is being discussed or investigated – and how it will be investigated. They may include:

- provision of information
- a description of the current situation under investigation
- a statement of the problem(s) to be solved
- alternatives to be considered
- possible solutions to be considered
- proposals to be examined
- a description of how the examination or investigation was carried out
- a description of research done or information collected
- the methodology and procedure of a research study.

Results/Findings

This section, within the main body of the report, may include:

- a clear summary of the main findings and/or results
- whether or not these results supported any hypotheses made
- a concise summary of the outcome of an investigation
- clearly labelled tables or diagrams if relevant.

Conclusion/Discussion

This must follow logically from the introduction and findings. The conclusion and discussion section or sections might include:

- interpretation and assessment of results/findings
- inferences drawn from findings, in the light of the aims and objectives stated earlier in the report
- suggested courses of action
- arguments and discussion
- proposals and recommendations.

Recommendations

A report might also include a separate section giving a list of recommendations (recommended actions arising from the report's findings). The recommendations should be clear and concise. They should be specific, not vague (perhaps including timescales for action and the names of people/departments responsible for carrying out the actions).

Acknowledgements, references and appendices

At the end of the report, there may need to be acknowledgements, a bibliography and/or appendices.

The acknowledgements would form a short section at the beginning or end of the report. It would list and thank any people or organizations that had helped in the production of the report (for example, by providing information or advice relevant to the report).

At the end of the report, all books and articles referred to in the report should be listed, in alphabetical order of authors' names, followed by the name of the book or journal, the year of publication, the volume number for journals, the publisher for books, and page references.

The purpose of an appendix is to provide detailed information which is not necessary for understanding the report, but which may be of interest to the reader. An appendix might contain tables of the full, detailed results and findings, of which summaries were presented in the 'Results' section. Or it might contain other documents relating to the report, or background information relevant to the report.

Ordering and linking of sections within a report

Because of their length and complexity, it is particularly important that reports should have a clear logical progression of ideas. To achieve this, the separate sections within the main body of the report need to be in a logical order. The following examples illustrate logical ordering in different types of report.

1 The logical thread might follow the pattern of a previous report, or the pattern of a document being responded to.
2 Information might be presented in order of importance, or in chronological order.
3 Sections might be ordered in the form of a logical argument, for example:

• proposal → advantages → disadvantages → evaluation
• alternatives → assessment → recommendations

- investigation → findings → conclusions
- problems → possible solutions → recommended solution
- current position → proposed changes → effects of changes.

4 There might be separate sections for each different topic or area that is covered in a report (e.g. different departments in a company, or different fields of activity on which information is being provided).

Note-taking for meetings or discussions

Note-taking is a common part of many jobs. It ranges from jotting down notes of informal discussions to formal minute-taking in meetings.

For many dyslexic people, note-taking is one of the hardest written tasks. It involves writing at speed, which is not easy for them. On top of that, it requires the note-takers to remember what is being said at the same time as writing it down - which can be very difficult for someone with short-term memory difficulties. And it also involves extended periods of focused concentration. As if all that weren't enough, people at meetings are notorious for wandering off the point, raising subjects out of order, interrupting each other and repeating themselves. (The last piece of behaviour, at least, can give dyslexic note-takers a breather.)

The following guidelines may help dyslexic employees to take notes more easily and efficiently.

Preparation

Given their difficulties with fast writing, sustained concentration and short-term memory, it is essential for dyslexic note-takers to prepare well before meetings. It will be far easier for them to take notes if they already know as much as possible about the subjects that will be discussed at the meeting. To do this, dyslexic people should:

- read and understand all background papers, agenda and agenda papers before the meeting
- read up any extra information they may need to help them follow the subjects to be discussed at the meeting
- make a note of any questions they might want to ask, or information they might want to obtain, at the meeting (if they have to participate as well as take notes, they are very likely to forget what they want to say or ask while they are engaged in note-taking)
- make a note of any decisions, recommendations or agreements that need to be made at the meeting.

It can also help greatly if dyslexic employees draw up a rough outline plan, before the meeting, of the subjects they expect the meeting to cover. This provides a framework for the notes, and the note-takers can then make their notes, as far as possible, to follow this outline plan. (If there is a formal Agenda paper, this will contain all the headings the notes will need, making a perfect outline plan for the minutes.)

Presentation and layout of notes

As always, clear layout is a great help to dyslexic people. This helps not only with taking the notes, but also in reading them later, in order to write them up. It is important that the notes taken at a meeting are as clear and easy to understand as possible, to enable note-takers to produce an accurate written report after the meeting.

The notes should be clearly laid out, with headings, subheadings and bullet points. There should be plenty of space to insert any information that comes up out of order in the meeting. (This can be achieved by writing in double spacing and leaving wide margins on both sides of the page.)

Taking the meeting notes

Note-takers should try not to write down everything that is said word-for-word. They should try instead to discern the important points (the main subjects; the key points and arguments; the actions agreed and decisions made; and the final outcomes of each subject under discussion). The pre-meeting plan and background reading will help the note-taker to know what is relevant and important. And speakers can always be asked to repeat their comments, if what they said turns out to be relevant after all.

Note-takers should also try to be alert to unnecessary rambling. It is common for people to veer off the point or repeat themselves during a meeting. It helps to notice when they do this, and not to waste time and energy taking notes of irrelevant discussions, repetitions and unnecessary padding.

To help keep up with the speakers, it is also important not to write out full words all the time, but to use as many abbreviations as possible (e.g. initials, or shortened forms of words). Note-takers should develop their own abbreviations for frequently occurring terms or words. They should also omit unnecessary linking words (e.g. 'Agreed rec foll acts to FC' rather than 'It was agreed that the following actions should be recommended to the Finance Committee').

It is also important for note-takers to be assertive when necessary during meetings. They should have the confidence to intervene to ensure that all the required subjects are covered; and all the appropriate decisions or recommendations are made. Dyslexic people should not be

---

BUDGET

- budg 2000 proposals discussed

- Agreed keep costs down

   Sales Dept

- bud proposals circulated & discussed

- agreed to all except public of new ad brochures

   (Old broch still OK)

   Accts Dept

- proposals circ and discussed

- NO to new computer syst

STAFF PAY INCS

- Agreed cost of liv inc

- Agreed merit inc max = 5%

Figure 12: Layout of notes using abbreviations

afraid to request clarification if they do not understand something that has been said – or to ask people to repeat something they have not had time to note fully. They should remember that it is difficult for anyone to keep up with note-taking, and not let any lack of confidence about their dyslexia stop them from taking control.

Contents of the notes

Notes of meetings should include the time, date and venue of the meeting, as well as its title or purpose. They also need to list the names of all people attending the meeting, along with their job titles, roles and affiliations where relevant (e.g. 'Head of Personnel Department', 'northeast regional representative', 'Director, Bloggs and Company', 'chairperson', 'secretary').

If there is a formal agenda, the notes will require subheadings for each agenda item. Note-takers should make sure they make notes on the outcomes required for each agenda item (e.g. decisions, agreements, recommendations, actions).

The notes should cover all the main points of the discussions on each topic, including:

- the main 'pros' and 'cons' put forward
- relevant facts and information given at the meeting
- the ideas or proposals rejected, and why
- the proposals accepted, and why
- matters agreed, considered, or noted
- recommendations made at the meeting
- future actions agreed at the meeting
- the outcome of each item discussed.

Format for formal agenda and minutes

Formal agenda and minutes require a standard structure and format. An example of such a format is given below. The structure and headings will be the same for both agenda and minutes: in effect, the minutes will 'mirror' the agenda.

Agenda and minutes: basic structure and contents

Heading. Name of committee; venue, time and date of meeting.

People at the meeting. List of names in alphabetic order, plus their role or attribution.

People unable to attend. Listed as above.

Apologies for absence. Record of any apologies received.

Minutes of the previous meeting. Minutes of previous meeting to be confirmed as a true record, with any corrections agreed.

Matters arising from the minutes. Any matters arising from the previous minutes that are not covered elsewhere in the agenda.

Chair's business. Opportunity for the chairperson to raise any important matters not covered elsewhere in the agenda (e.g. last-minute issues or developments that arose after the agenda was circulated).

Main items for discussion. Items arranged in order of importance, to allow time for full consideration to be given to the most important matters.

Regular topics. Topics routinely covered at every meeting, for example regular reports from standing sub-committees; treasurer's report.

Periodic topics. For example, annual budget.

Any other business. Any other items of important business, at the discretion of the Chair.

Date of the next meeting.

* * * * * *

For formal meetings, each item in the agenda should state clearly what outcome is required (e.g. 'To agree...', 'To consider...', 'To approve...', 'To make recommendations on...', 'To note...', 'To discuss and agree actions on...'.)

The minutes should reflect the agenda, and state clearly the outcome of each item from the agenda (e.g. 'It was <u>agreed</u> that the following actions should be carried out before the next meeting...', 'It was <u>agreed</u> <u>to recommend</u> to the Finance Committee that...', 'The committee <u>noted</u> that...'.

All actions to be taken should also be clearly recorded, along with the people responsible for undertaking the actions.

As the minutes will serve as an official record of the meeting, as well as a working document for future actions, it will be useful to record not only the decisions reached, but also a succinct record of the reasons for the decisions (e.g. the main thread of argument and discussion leading to the decision, alternative ideas discussed, ideas rejected and why).

Chapter 14
Reading and remembering work documents

It is not easy to find a job that does not involve some degree of reading. Most jobs at least require the reading of short memos or e-mails. Many involve the reading of lengthy and complex reports and other documents. Even jobs that might be thought to require no reading, such as motor repair, often depend on the ability to read complex instruction manuals. One dyslexic person thought he had solved all his problems by getting a job as a chef. He found to his dismay that he had to read a bank of information about hygiene and health in the kitchen, and he had to decipher and read long and complex words, such as the names of various bacteria found on food, and the foreign names for food on menus.

Dyslexic people often have difficulty both in reading and remembering written text. Their sequencing difficulties and their problems with word and letter recognition make the process of reading slow and arduous. And their short-term memory difficulties make it hard for them to understand and remember what they are reading.

In some jobs, the volume and complexity of reading may become overwhelming to dyslexic employees, and they may feel tempted to give up the battle. However, there are some strategies and techniques that can help them to improve their reading speed and memory and enable them to cope.

Of course there will always be other jobs that might be easier for dyslexic people. And they are so often advised by well-meaning friends and family to take the easier option. But if their heart is in a particular job, and if they have the underlying talent for that job, they can learn to cope with it in spite of their dyslexic difficulties. The work may always take them a little longer to do, but it will become much easier. The following case study illustrates this. Its message is: 'Do not give up'.

Katherine, a newly qualified law graduate, had always wanted to be a lawyer. She had insisted on studying law, against the advice of her family and friends, who knew how badly her dyslexia affected her reading, writing and memory. Katherine had recently started her first job in a busy solicitors' practice. She had a sharp, enquiring mind, and found she loved the challenge of legal work.

Katherine had succeeded in getting her law degree only by putting in many extra hours poring over lecture notes and legal textbooks late into the night. But there was no time for this in her new job, with its very heavy workload and constant pressure. She had to read many complex and detailed legal documents every day. Much of the reading matter was in close print with very poor layout. She also had to read difficult expert witness reports, which frequently contained complex calculations of costs and detailed tables of statistics. Because of the sheer volume of reading Katherine had to do, her desk was always piled high with files, reports and legal books, which made her feel confused and stressed.

Katherine's as yet untackled dyslexic difficulties meant that her reading speed and memory skills were not adequate to cope with the mass of complex routine reading that was an essential part of her job. She took papers home to read and came into work tired every morning. In spite of this, the reading continued to pile up. Her enjoyment of the job was becoming swamped by the ever-increasing piles of unread papers. She was stressed and exhausted most of the time, and began to wonder whether her struggles to get her law degree had all been a waste of time. There were many times when she came close to handing in her notice and giving up her dream of becoming a successful lawyer.

Although her employers were sympathetic about her dyslexic difficulties, they simply did not have the spare time themselves to help her as much as they would have liked. Then one day – to her embarrassment – she collapsed in tears during a meeting with her boss about her lack of progress in her work. But this awkward moment proved to be the turning point. It showed her boss the full extent and effect of her dyslexic difficulties, and he decided to find the time and funds to help her. He asked staff to present work documents in a clearer, easier-to-read format and to highlight key words and phrases. He took time each day to help Katherine summarize and scan legal texts and to guide her to the relevant sections to be read. He also arranged for Katherine to tape meetings, discussions and oral instructions, and he began to take the time to explain new jobs carefully to her.

On top of this, Katherine's boss got the firm to fund weekly training for her, to tackle her severe dyslexic difficulties in word and letter recognition – training she should ideally have received when she was much younger. Katherine's training also included ways to improve her memory for written text, and she learned to put her strong visual skills to work to help her memory. (She had training in writing skills too, but that is the subject of another chapter.)

It took time, but slowly Katherine's reading and memory skills improved. As they did, the size of the piles of paper on her desk began to decrease, and she became steadily more in control of her job. She still has some way to go, but she is coping. At last, she is beginning to enjoy doing the legal work she loves. Her employers are well satisfied with her progress, and they are beginning to see – and to benefit from – her true potential and legal talents.

The job described above is just about the worst possible scenario for a dyslexic employee, but it is not unusual. Many administrative or managerial jobs also involve a large volume of reading of letters, reports and meeting papers. For dyslexic employees in such jobs, it is essential to develop all the techniques and strategies they can to combat their dyslexic difficulties with reading. It is also important for them to remember – however impossible it may seem – that with the help of appropriate strategies and techniques, they will be able to cope with heavy loads of written texts. There are many successful dyslexic lawyers, administrators and managers to prove the point.

This chapter covers ways to improve reading speed, accuracy and memory – from tackling the underlying decoding and sequencing problems to using a range of techniques to help improve memory for written text. It also includes some advice on reading complex visual arrays, such as graphs and tables of statistics. It begins with the memory skills, and how to use all of the brain to help remember things.

Remembering written text

Remembering written text is often best achieved by not trying to force oneself to remember. This only causes stress, and research has shown that stress is one of the worst conditions for memory. Added to dyslexic difficulties, it can make simply comprehending written text seem impossible – let alone remembering it. So, rather than trying to cram facts into their heads, and becoming stressed when they will not stay there, there are other methods that dyslexic people can use to let the information sink more naturally and easily into their memory. Among other things, these simple techniques will work to activate both sides of the brain – particularly the right hemisphere, which may be well developed in many dyslexic people; this side of the brain 'specializes' in visual material, which is particularly helpful to memory.

The following list outlines a range of techniques that can be applied to any form of written text, from short letters to lengthy office reports. Each technique in the list is covered in more detail later in the chapter.

- Working from clearly presented and visually attractive material.
- Marking and highlighting poorly presented material.
- Getting a general overview before reading the text in detail..
- Highlighting or underlining key words to produce a summary.
- Making summaries in the form of spider charts or mind-maps.
- Writing key words or phrases in the margin.
- Thinking about – and understanding – what is being read.
- Using memory strategies such as association and visualization.
- Taking regular breaks and working in stages.
- Reviewing what has been read at regular intervals.

Of course, all this might seem very time-consuming, particularly to the dyslexic person in a busy job, to whom time is crucial. In fact, it usually saves time. Going through a long report once – slowly, thoughtfully and actively – is usually quicker than rushing through it quickly over and over again, becoming more and more stressed and remembering very little. It is surprising how much can be remembered simply by reading with thought and attention, making links with other things, bringing the subject to life in visual imagination, highlighting key words and using spider charts or mind-maps to aid memory. (Full details on the use of mind-maps to help memory, and other memory techniques, can be found in the range of books written by Tony Buzan; see Buzan (1982) for examples.)

This is not only more pleasant to do than straightforward 'cramming', it is also a more intelligent method of remembering. Forced learning will eventually get the facts into memory, but it is memory without thinking. Only the bare facts will be recorded, not the deeper understanding and additional ideas that arise when using the techniques listed above. Using the following techniques will help anyone to remember better, but for dyslexic people, they are especially relevant.

Presentation of material

The presentation of material has already been discussed in earlier chapters, which show how much easier it is to understand text that is well presented. But good presentation does more than help with understanding – it also makes it easier to remember. A pleasant visual layout will stimulate the right side of the brain, which will help the memory. Dyslexic employees should consider asking their boss and work colleagues to produce well laid out documents with spaces, colours, bulleted lists, diagrams and key words highlighted in bold text. They could also request instructions to be produced in the form of flow charts whenever possible.

If there is a choice, dyslexic people should always go for the better-presented document. If not, they will find that marking the document themselves will help them to remember it. Simply ruling lines between paragraphs or sections can make a big difference, by producing a basic pattern as well as dividing the text into smaller chunks. Highlighting headings in one colour and key words in another can also help memory, as can drawing boxes around sections of text. These text markings can be particularly helpful in documents such as detailed instruction manuals or work procedures.

Getting an overview

Dyslexic people will find that it is much easier to remember text if they begin by getting an overview of the contents and structure of the whole document before they read it in detail. (To a large extent, marking the text as described above achieves this.) To get an overview:

- first skim rapidly through the whole document to get a general idea of its subject matter and direction; this does not mean skimming the entire document, just reading the contents page, the main section headings, and the main introduction and conclusion (which often contain a succinct summary of the whole document)
- then skim through each section, looking at subheadings, bulleted lists, emboldened text, etc.
- look also at the introductory and concluding paragraphs in each section.

Reports are particularly amenable to this sort of overviewing; they usually contain plenty of bold headings and subheadings, as well as a brief summary of the whole report at the beginning, and a list of conclusions or recommendations at the end. (For overloaded dyslexic employees, simply reading these will often provide an adequate picture of the contents of the whole report.)

Once they have got a general impression of the overall scope and gist of a document, dyslexic employees will find that they will remember the details far more easily when they go on to read the full document.

Making a summary

To remember what is read, the very least that is required is a bit of time and thought. Summarizing the contents of a document forces the reader to think about what is being said, and so acts as a memory aid in itself. This does not mean writing out a shortened version of a document. Instead, a summary can be made by underlining or highlighting key words or phrases in a document. Or it can be made in the form of a spider diagram or a mind-map – visual formats that many dyslexic people find particularly helpful to memory.

Underlining, highlighting and marking text

Making a summary by means of highlights, underlines and margin notes gives readers a task to do, rather than simply ploughing their way through a complex document and trying to force themselves to remember it. Because they often find reading a real chore, dyslexic people may feel that having to underline key words as well would make the chore even more unpleasant. But when they try it, they often find that underlining is less tedious and more stimulating than straightforward reading. (It is certainly more useful, as it provides a neat embedded summary within the text so that the reader does not need to go through the entire document again.) And it can serve as a powerful memory aid, as it forces the reader to think about and understand the text. It is especially helpful in documents such as instruction manuals or work procedures, which may need to be reread frequently.

When they first perform this task, dyslexic people may feel uncertain about what key words to underline. It may help if they think of it as reducing the text to note form, and underline just the main nouns (things) and verbs (action words). They should also omit extra 'frills', for instance underlining only one example instead of a whole list of examples. They should try to be decisive – underlining what seem to be key words rather than spending ages in inner debate. They can then check their underlining by going back after each section and reading only the underlined words to see if they make sense. At this stage, they can make any necessary changes, underlining more words or rubbing out unnecessary words. Once the check has been done, the underlined words can be highlighted, to provide colour and permanence. (This checking process also serves as a review, and helps to lay down the information in the long-term memory.)

It also helps to write down a word or phrase in the margin beside each paragraph or subsection to sum up its core meaning. This aids memory by making the reader really think about the core meaning of each paragraph. It also provides a useful set of subheadings in the margin to act as triggers to the contents.

HIGHLIGHTS/ MARGIN NOTES	Making a <u>summary</u> by means of <u>highlights,</u> <u>underlines</u> and <u>margin notes</u> gives readers a <u>task</u> to do, <u>rather than</u> simply <u>ploughing</u> their way <u>through</u> a complex <u>document</u> and trying to force themselves to remember it.
WHAT TO UNDERLINE	When they <u>first</u> peform this task, dyslexic people <u>may feel uncertain</u> about <u>what</u> key words <u>to</u> <u>underline</u>. It <u>may help</u> if they think of it as <u>reducing</u> the text <u>to note form</u>, and <u>underlining</u> just the <u>main</u> <u>nouns</u> (things) <u>and verbs</u> (action words).

Figure 13: Marking text.

Making a summary in pattern form

Many dyslexic people have strong visual abilities and therefore find it far easier to remember from patterns such as spider diagrams or flow charts. A simple spider diagram, for example, preferably incorporating different colours, will present a clear visual pattern that will stimulate the right side of the brain and enhance memory. It also has the advantage of displaying the whole summary on one page, allowing the dyslexic person to see the links and relationships between different aspects. It provides a clear summary, in a visually attractive form, that is quick to review at a glance. Most dyslexics find this much easier to read and remember than ordinary text. (See Figure 14).

Other patterns can be used. For instance, a flow chart with boxes and arrows, or a 'family tree' chart, can also provide clear visual patterns to make summaries.

Stimulating memory with active thought

Something else that can greatly enhance memory is simply to *think* about what is being read. While the highlighting or pattern making is being done, readers should try to think actively about the text - to consider and assess it; to wonder about it; to think how it applies to them. While reading text, dyslexic employees should try to do the following things.

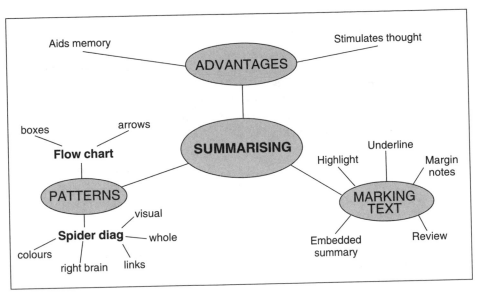

Figure 14: Spider diagram summary.

- **Consider** carefully what they are reading: its meaning and purpose; how it links with other things; how it applies to the real world and how it affects their job.
- **Question** what they are reading: for example, how useful it is; whether it makes sense; whether it is workable.
- **Judge** what they are reading: for example, whether or not they agree with it; what its good and bad points are; what criticisms they have of the ideas expressed; and whether they can think of better ideas.
- **Understand** what they are reading. This is very important, as once the thread is lost, it can become almost impossible to remember. If a text is not understood, it is important to find out the meaning, perhaps by asking someone else at work.

All this thinking forces readers to make links between the text they are reading and other things they know. This leads on to the next aspect of remembering written text – the use of two valuable memory techniques: association and visualization.

Association

Aiding memory by making links or associations with other things is one of the oldest and most effective memory techniques. In effect, the more links that are made between what is being read and what the reader already knows, the easier it will be to recall the information at a later date.

Many dyslexic people have active imaginations and find it hard to keep their mind from shooting off on to associated ideas – and here is a situation where they can put this tendency to good use. While reading, they should (within reason) allow their mind to think 'around the subject' – to let the text spark off related ideas that spring to mind as they read; and to deliberately try to think of associated ideas, and to make links with other things they know. (Of course, if the mind wanders off on to a totally different subject, it is necessary to bring it back. But as long as the associated idea is directly linked to what is being read, it will help to hold it in the memory.)

Associations might arise, for example, if people simply think of how the reading matter relates to them or their job; or of what it reminds them of, how it applies to the real world and how it links with other parts of the document.

It is also helpful to make clear and deliberate links between each paragraph or section of the document by noticing how they relate to each other and how one leads on to the other.

Story-line associations

If a dyslexic employee has a detailed list to be remembered in the right order, such as a work procedure or a set of instructions, it can be very effective to make use of deliberately contrived associations - to create a 'story-line' of ideas associated with each item in the list. The story-line provides natural links between each item on the list, and the vividness of the images help to hold them in the memory. This exercise requires imagination and visualization – both right-brain skills that many dyslexics have developed strongly as a strategy to help tackle their dyslexic difficulties. The more exaggerated and humorous the story, the easier it will be to remember.

Paul, a dyslexic taxi driver who wanted to drive a black cab, found that this technique helped him immensely to learn 'The Knowledge'. His dyslexic difficulties made the learning of lists of street names an enormous battle. He used visual storylines to help him learn the most difficult ones. He would take a list of streets, make up a visual image associated with each one, and link them together in order in a story. For example, he might have to learn the following street names in order: Sydney Street, Woodberry

Road, Hatley Lane, Myddleton Street, Curzon Road, Nightingale Road and Windermere Avenue. He would have fun making up a story-line something like the one that follows.

He pictured his friend **Sidney** in a **wood**, picking **berries** from the trees (a most unlikely image, since Sidney was definitely a 'city-person' – but the more incongruous the image, the easier it is to remember). He then imagined the sun bursting through between the branches of the trees, and pictured Sidney putting on a huge, floppy straw **hat** (<u>Hat</u>ley Road). The picture of the usually smart-suited Sidney in a straw hat was particularly amusing and striking.

Then, to Sidney's utter surprise and delight, he walked through another clump of trees and came upon a **town** right in the **middle** of the wood (Myddleton Street). Paul imagined Sidney's glee at finding himself in a town again.

The next street – Curzon Street – baffled Paul. He could think of no image for it, so he decided to leave just that one to the memory. However, to remind himself that there was a 'missing link' here, he imagined Sidney suddenly beginning to wonder why on earth there was a town in the middle of the wood, and pictured a huge, neon-lit **question mark** appearing on the top of his straw hat.

Paul then imagined the neon question mark attracting a flock of **nightingales**, which perched all around the brim of Sidney's straw hat, singing loudly together. A sudden gust of **wind** (<u>Wind</u>ermere Avenue) then blew through the trees, blowing away the straw hat, nightingales, question mark and all.

It took Paul some time, at first, to dream up stories like this, but he soon became adept at it. It was more fun than simply sitting and memorizing, and it enabled him to learn and retain the difficult sequences of streets.

The following imaginative story-line was invented by a dyslexic research scientist, who had to keep up with all the latest research by reading piles of journal articles every day. The aim of this particular story-line was to help her remember the list of techniques that would help her remember written text! Her story, reproduced below, may help readers of this chapter to remember those memory techniques too.

List of ways to remember text	*Story-line image*
1 Use well-presented colourful material	Imagine an artist beside a window in an attic studio, painting a **vivid brightly coloured picture**
2 Get an overview	The artist glances out of the studio window and looks out **over the view of the city** at night
3 Highlight key words	The city scene is glittering with bright-coloured **neon signs** (highlights)
4 Make spider diagrams	As the artist gazes at the city lights, a huge **spider** falls from the ceiling right on to his painting
5 Make associations	The spider **reminds** the artist of a film he once saw about deadly tarantula spiders
6 Use visualization	His **imagination** runs wild, and he **pictures** his attic studio filling up with tarantulas
7 Take breaks	He panics at the picture he's imagined and rushes **away from his work** to have a drink to calm him down. After the drink, he feels braver, and goes back to do more work on his painting
8 Review what has been read at regular	For the next month, whenever the artist goes out, he tells people the story of the spider that frightened him
9 Use sound equipment	When he doesn't go out, he uses the **telephone** to call friends and tell them the spider story

This sort of association may take a little time to build up, but the visual and imaginative skills of many dyslexics may make it relatively easy for them compared with non-dyslexics. And once it has been done, the list should remain firmly in the memory in the right order. (This technique can also be used to make links between key words written in the margin of each paragraph or section of a document.)

Visualization

It will be clear from the above example that another technique that enhances memory is visualization. Visual imagery can be one of the strongest memory aids.

Wherever possible, people should try to picture in their minds what they are reading, and put themselves in the picture if they can. The images should be as interesting, active and vivid as possible, ideally incorporating a range of the senses: sound, smell and touch, as well as vision. As with the story-line associations, the more colourful, exaggerated or humorous the image, the easier it will be to remember.

The important thing is to make sure the image is strongly linked to the text, otherwise the image will stay in the memory, but the reader may forget what it is supposed to remind him of. For example, to remember that there are tiny bones in the ear called the 'hammer', the 'anvil' and the 'stirrup', a dyslexic person might imagine a tiny blacksmith's shop making a huge din inside his ear, with the blacksmith **hammering** a horseshoe on his **anvil**, while the horse's **stirrups** jangle to and fro. *It is essential to imagine that this visual image is very noisy and right inside the ear to make the link with the bones in the ear.*

Dyslexic employees may feel that it is not so easy to concoct such a striking visual image in relation to work documents. But with a little inventiveness, some very dull work documents or procedures can be brought to life in the imagination. If this is not possible, it can help simply to imagine the work situation in action. One dyslexic accountant, for example, was faced with having to remember a detailed new computing procedure which he had to help his staff put into action. As he read the procedures, he imagined himself and his staff actually doing each stage of the job, envisaged their reactions to the new procedures and pictured himself trying to explain to them why the changes had been made. He imagined their confusion, their resistance, and their mistakes in carrying out the new procedures. He pictured everything going wrong, and then imagined them putting things right. When it came to the real-life implementation of the new procedures, he found he remembered what to do far more clearly than he had expected.

The dyslexic lawyer mentioned at the beginning of this chapter found that it helped her greatly to remember past judgements from legal books if she brought the court cases to life in her mind like a television film, imagining what the judge and the participants looked like, what they said and did during the case, and their emotional reactions to the judgement.

Taking breaks

As mentioned in Chapter 9, without regular short breaks, all mental performance, including memory, gets progressively worse over time, and the amount remembered will drop dramatically after a while.

On average, the most efficient length of time for reading and remembering ranges between around 30 minutes and an hour. (The time will vary depending on the state of tiredness, the difficulty of the text, etc. It will be shorter than average for dyslexic people, who need to put more concentration into decoding the words.) Most people can tell when they need a break because their concentration begins to flag and the reading begins to feel more and more arduous. When they reach this point, they will remember very little, and it is advisable to take a ten-minute break – or to move on to a different, less arduous task for a while if a break is not possible.

To ensure regular breaks are taken, dyslexic readers could set small subgoals in a document, reading just a few pages, or a section of a report, at a time and taking a short break in between each chunk.

Reviewing

If it is necessary to remember something over time, readers will need to review what they have read at regular intervals. This will help to lay down the information in the long-term memory. A routine pattern of reviewing is the best way to achieve this.

* Skim-reading the section of text that has just been highlighted, or summarised in pattern form, will serve as the first review. (*It is not necessary to try to force it into the memory, just to read through the highlighted bits or the spider diagram.*)
* The next review should be at the end of the day, simply reading over what has been highlighted or summarized during the day.
* The week's reading should then be read over in the same way at the end of the week, and the month's reading at the end of the month.

All of these techniques may seem time-consuming, but once the dyslexic reader becomes familiar with them, they can be done quite quickly and automatically. To recap:

1 Get a quick overview.
2 Mark the text to improve presentation.
3 Make a summary with highlights or patterns.
4 At the same time as the above, think about the text, visualize it and make associations.
5 Take breaks.
6 Do a review.

The alternative is to plough through the text again and again, trying to force it into the memory, and probably remembering very little. In contrast, doing the things described above will activate different parts of the brain and help the information to stay in the memory *without actually trying to do it*. On top of this, dyslexic people should use whatever physical aids they can to help them remember, such as sound equipment.

Using sound equipment to aid memory

Dyslexic employees can also use sound equipment to help them remember, as well as to save them the time-consuming task of deciphering written material. Many dyslexic employees find that it helps memory if they read a written document on to a tape and listen back to it.

For reading text from a computer, the use of a text-to-voice software package will allow dyslexic employees to listen to the text as well as read it, which often helps them to remember it.

Some dyslexic people find that simply reading text aloud to themselves helps them remember it. Others find this an extra distraction. Each person should explore to see what works for them. If reading aloud or listening to tapes or voice software helps, dyslexic staff should ask their employers if there is a vacant room where they can listen or read aloud, such as an unused meeting room.

Dyslexic workers could also ask their employers to provide them with tape recorders and dictaphones, and request permission to tape meetings and discussions. They can then listen to the meeting later, rather than read the meeting notes or minutes.

Simply talking about things also helps people to remember them. Whenever possible, dyslexic employees should discuss work documents with their colleagues.

Tackling the underlying difficulties

There is one more thing that can improve dyslexic people's memory for written material, and that is tackling their underlying difficulties with word recognition and decoding. Whatever the degree of reading difficulty, the underlying problems with sequencing and with word and letter discrimination will effectively hinder memory for text. Because dyslexic people are having to put extra effort and concentration into decoding the words and letters, their brains are often too overloaded to remember what they are reading on top of deciphering it. So working to improve reading speed and accuracy often automatically makes it easier to remember what is being read.

Reading speed and accuracy

Dyslexic people's problems with reading speed and accuracy can cause them many problems at work. The extra time it takes them to decipher documents leaves them with less time to deal with other parts of their job. Reading aloud from written text in a meeting can be a nightmare.

At worst, a dyslexic person may have very severe problems with basic word and letter recognition, making reading extremely slow and inaccurate. Their sequencing difficulties will make them muddle up the bits of a word, and lose track of the sense of a sentence. And it is not uncommon for reading difficulties of this degree of severity to persist into adulthood if the dyslexia was not diagnosed and tackled at school. These people will very likely have been forced to seek employment in jobs well below their potential. And they may still have problems, as most jobs involve at least some reading.

Other dyslexic people will have less pronounced reading difficulties, but will still find reading an arduous and time-consuming task. These people – such as the newly graduated lawyer mentioned at the beginning of this chapter – will often have fought their way through the education system by putting in many extra hours of study. They frequently find themselves seriously overloaded and stressed when they enter employment.

For those with severe difficulties, it is sensible to begin 'at the beginning', by dealing with the underlying difficulties. They should seek specialist training to build up their knowledge of word and letter sounds, including perceptual and discrimination exercises in letter-strings and word-bits. This is hard work and may take time, but with perseverance, most dyslexic adults are able to improve their reading speed and accuracy dramatically, once they have developed their basic word and letter recognition and decoding skills. They also need to work to become familiar with the various common word-bits that crop up again and again in different words, and to practise word building and word division with them (for example, the common prefixes such as 'trans-', 'pre-', 'com-'; suffixes such as '-ly', '-ness', '-ity', '-ive'; and common word roots such as 'duct', 'vert', 'gress').

On top of this, there are other ways for dyslexic people to improve the speed and accuracy of their reading. Some of these are outlined below.

Reading more

Many dyslexic people avoid reading unless they have to do it. This is a mistake, since the more they read, the more familiar they will become with words and letters, and the better their reading will become. To build up their reading practice, it is a good idea for dyslexic people to set themselves reading goals outside working time.

Many dyslexic readers will throw up their hands in horror at the thought of doing more reading, but the goal need not be demanding. Indeed, it is best if it is not, because too difficult a goal on top of a busy job can be demotivating. So the idea is to start small, with 10 or 15 minutes a day of reading something that interests them. And it need not be a work document – a short magazine or newspaper article a day, perhaps, or a page or two of a book is fine. The aim is simply to build up reading time and practice, and the motivation to do this will be higher if the subject matter is light or interesting.

If it is kept up over time, this extra reading practice will, of course, help all reading, including more complex work documents. To provide motivation and give a sense of achievement, it is a good idea to write down the daily reading goals on a chart or in a diary, and tick them off when they are met.

In addition, since many jobs require a degree of background reading (which dyslexic employees often avoid, making them less informed than they could be about their job), it is a good idea for them to extend their reading practice to cover this. They might consider setting aside a short time – perhaps a half an hour at the beginning of each working day – to read at least some of the background reading material in their in-tray.

Noticing the separate bits in words

It is common for dyslexic people to lose their place in long words, reading the bits out of order, and adding or omitting bits. This causes confusion and the need for rereading, and takes up valuable time. They also tend to take wild guesses, instead of reading what is actually on the page. Sometimes this strategy works, and this saves time – but often the guesses are wrong, and the sense of the sentence disappears with the wrong guess.

To tackle this, it helps if dyslexic people get into the habit of noticing the separate bits in words, particularly the common bits, and read through the words carefully, one bit at a time. The aim is to look for what is actually there, not what they expect to be there, and to tackle the sequencing errors by taking long words slowly, systematically scanning through each bit in order. At first, this may be difficult for dyslexics; they will find it hard to keep the sequence, and the temptation to guess will be strong. It may help to imagine that the brain is a computer scanner, highlighting each word-bit, one by one. With time and practice, they will become steadily more adept, and steadily faster and more accurate at deciphering long words.

Noticing the ends of words

Errors at the ends of words are particularly common with dyslexia. Dyslexic readers should therefore pay especial attention to word-ends (such as '-ed' and '-s'), as these can make quite a difference to the meaning.

Watching out for small words

Dyslexic people often skip over small words (such as 'in', 'at' or 'no'). Although small, these words are often important to the meaning. Making a conscious decision to notice small words can help a lot in under-standing the meaning, and thus save time.

Keeping place in the text

Another thing that dyslexic people have trouble with is keeping their place in the text. Simply tracking their place down the margin with a finger or a pen while they read can help a lot, and save time spent constantly seeking for the place. It can also help to run a finger or pen under and along each line, just ahead of what is being read. This usually serves to 'pull the focus along the line' and can help to speed up reading.

Dyslexic people will also find Post-it index stickers helpful to mark their place when they take a break from reading. These can be stuck at the side of the paragraph where the reading broke off, and then moved on, over and over again to mark each new break. This will save them repeated time-consuming searches for their position within a page each time they resume reading. (These movable index stickers are also useful to mark places in a document that may need to be referred to, for example in a meeting or discussion. Dyslexic employees can suffer great difficulty and anxiety trying to find a particular piece of text while being watched by other participants in a meeting, and the index stickers can solve this awkward problem.)

Practising reading in chunks

Instead of reading one word at a time, it often helps to focus on 'meaning units' of two or three words at a time (e.g. *'in the morning'*, *'after a while'* or *'as a result'*). With practice, this can help greatly to increase reading speed. It means that, instead of stopping at every single word, the reader is taking in bigger chunks at every 'look'. Doing this is not nearly as diffi-cult as it might at first sound to dyslexic readers. Using the technique mentioned above of running the finger ahead can help. (Of course, long complex words will still need to be read separately, bit by bit.)

Marking the document

Instead of trying to read pages of dense text, many dyslexic people find it helps to divide up the text visually before they read it. Even simply ruling a horizontal line across the page between each paragraph or section makes the text appear much less daunting. It also provides a series of visual subgoals to progress through.

Noticing the visual pattern and shape of individual words

Each word has its own shape, and some dyslexic people find that noticing this helps them to read the words. They should also notice the recurring patterns formed by common word-bits such as 'pre-' and '-able' (reli*able*; us*able*; wash*able*; *pre*sent*able*; *pre*pare; *pre*tend.)

Taking breaks from reading

A break every 30 to 45 minutes will refresh concentration. This is particularly important for those dyslexic people with severe word-recognition difficulties, who have to use a lot of concentration to read. Without regular breaks, their reading speed and accuracy will deteriorate further.

Using reading aids

Dyslexic employees should take advantage of any physical aids that might make their reading easier. As well as helping memory, auditory equipment can save dyslexic people the effort of decoding written text. The use of text-to-speech computer software to enable people to listen to text on the computer rather than read it has already been mentioned. The use of this and other auditory devices such as voice mail can make a dyslexic employee's life a great deal easier. Dyslexic employees could also ask their boss or work colleagues to produce instructions or documents in oral form on tapes whenever possible. And they could ask to take tape-recordings of meetings, discussions and training courses.

Some dyslexic people's reading difficulties are compounded by the glare from white paper, or by the experience of blurring or apparent movement of print on a page. These problems can be eased by the use of non-reflective, transparent, coloured plastic overlays on documents; by copying documents on to tinted paper; and by changing the background colours and text colours on computer screens. At the very least, these will reduce glare; for some dyslexic people, they can noticeably enhance the ease of reading. Irlen prescription tinted glasses or overlays should also be investigated, as they can be a great help with certain types of dyslexia.

However helpful these aids may be, it will be very difficult for anyone to escape unaided reading completely at work. For this reason, the various methods covered in this chapter to improve reading speed, accuracy and memory are well worth practising. Different techniques will work better for different individuals, depending on their own learning styles. Each method will contribute to making reading easier for dyslexic people, so they should try out each one and either use them all, or select the ones that seem to help them most.

Reading graphs and tables

In spite of the visual strengths of many dyslexic people, and their tendency to find visual patterns easier to read, many of them have serious difficulty with very complex or detailed visual arrays, such as tables of statistics, graphs or critical path analyses. These types of presentation can include so much detail, often densely packed together in small print, that they are particularly confusing to dyslexic people (indeed, to most people, dyslexic or not). There are several ways to make these visual arrays easier to read.

Colours and lines

First, there is the usual trick - using colours and lines to highlight and divide up the contents. This could include highlighting the title and the column headings of a table in different colours, and drawing clear lines between columns and rows. The colours and lines can make a mass of closely packed, confusing information 'fall into shape', form patterns and begin to make sense.

On graphs or bar-charts, clear horizontal and vertical lines can be drawn across the graph or chart from the main values on the axes. Different curves on the graph (or bars on a bar-chart) can be given different colours. On a critical path analysis, dates can be highlighted, vertical lines can be drawn to separate each week, and different activities can be given different colours.

As always, the marking and colouring does more than make the presentation easier to read – the action of marking also makes the reader take note of the main headings and subheadings, and this helps them to make sense of the array.

Overview

Second, it helps to begin by getting a clear overview of the array, by reading the main title, all the row and column headings and subheadings, and the titles of each axis on a graph, etc.

Scanning

Third, for things like tables of statistics, which do not present a clear visual overview or pattern, it is important to scan the array carefully and systematically, to 'sweep' methodically through the data from left to right and top to bottom (or along one column, row or section at time) and to take in each piece of information one at a time. If this is not done, it is very easy to miss some of the information and fail to get the full picture. And it is common for dyslexic people, when faced with this sort of complex presentation, to skip erratically from place to place all over the document, covering some sections many times and others not at all. Doing this, they will inevitably miss out on some of the information.

Thinking

Finally, as with reading written text, it helps to think about what is being presented: what it means, how it relates to other parts of the display, etc. (For example, on a graph or table of data over time, to think about what may be causing the dips or rises; or on a critical path analysis, to note which activities overlap and when, and consider what problems this could cause.)

Chapter 15
General oral skills and interaction

Dyslexia does not necessarily affect oral skills. Many dyslexic people are extremely competent at expressing themselves orally. Others, however, have similar difficulties with oral expression as they have with writing. They find it very hard to convert their thoughts and ideas into spoken words; and their ideas get muddled and come out in the wrong order.

Of course, oral interaction involves listening as well as speaking, and dyslexic people often have difficulties in this area too. They can find it difficult to sustain their concentration and focus their attention while listening to people talking. This makes it hard for them to keep up with telephone conversations, discussions or speeches. Their short-term memory difficulties can also make them forget what has been said.

In addition, oral expression is particularly susceptible to lack of confidence. Speaking – whether in public or just interacting with colleagues – means having to come up with the right words on the spot, with no chance for the checking and redrafting that can be done with written work. This can sap the confidence of most people. For those with dyslexia who are unsure of their oral skills, speaking in meetings or work discussions with colleagues can become a terrifying experience.

These difficulties with oral interactions can cause serious problems for dyslexic people at work. Most jobs involve daily interactions and discussions with colleagues, as well as frequent speaking on the telephone. They also involve frequent oral instructions, particularly at the start of new jobs. And many types of work that do not involve much writing require a great deal of oral interaction, for example the work of the telephonist, the receptionist or the salesperson. At higher levels of responsibility, employees are usually expected to attend and participate in meetings, and to give formal oral presentations from time to time. Whatever the job or the level of seniority, it is difficult to avoid oral activities at work. It is therefore very important for people to tackle their oral difficulties as well as their written ones.

Many of the techniques to improve oral expression are the same as those for written and other work: preparation, organization, going slowly and using the imagination. These have already been covered in earlier chapters, and so will be referred to only briefly here.

This chapter covers a range of different ways to help improve oral interaction at work, with references to relevant chapters in other parts of the book. It looks first at the preparation and planning for oral interactions and at ways to build confidence before speaking. It goes on to cover the process of talking itself, and ends with ways to improve listening skills.

The preparation

It is essential to prepare for most oral interactions – from the ten-minute meeting with the boss to the formal oral presentation before an audience. The preparation is very much the same as that for written work. Planning a short talk with the boss might be similar to planning for writing a memo; and planning a formal oral presentation will be similar to planning a written report. (See Chapters 12 and 13.)

Informal discussions

For an informal discussion or a meeting with the boss, it is important for dyslexic people to take a little time beforehand to jot down the points they want to raise. Their difficulties with concentration and short-term memory can easily make them forget some of the things they wanted to say. And interactive discussions tend to veer off in unpredictable directions before a person has said all they want to say on a particular subject. Having a card listing each point they want to raise looks efficient, and it allows dyslexic people to refer to the card as a reminder, to cross off points covered, and to check at the end of the discussion and make any points or ask any questions that have been missed.

Formal talks

For a formal speech, the planning is an important and more lengthy process. As for report planning, it should include getting the whole picture on a spider diagram, checking that all aspects of the subject have been covered, clustering the ideas into groups and ordering them to form a logical thread. The talk should then be written up in note form on cards. (In most cases, cards are preferable to sheets of paper; it is easy for dyslexic people to lose their place on a sheet of paper and if a speaker is nervous, the sheet of paper will quiver and betray the nervousness.)

However, even with cards, it can be difficult for dyslexic people to read aloud and to keep their place while talking. And losing the place in mid-speech can cause embarrassment and destroy confidence. To make this easier, the speech should be very clearly laid out on the cards, with headings in capitals, subheadings, bullet points, colours and spaces. It also helps to draw horizontal lines between separate points, to help people keep their place on the cards. The cards should be clearly numbered in case they are muddled or dropped. Even better, reproducing the cards as a summary of the speech on slides or overhead projections will be a great help to the dyslexic speaker as well as to the audience.

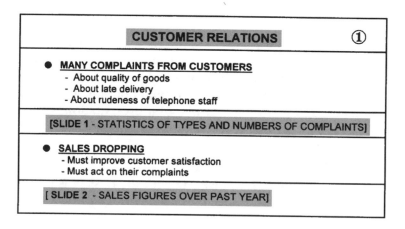

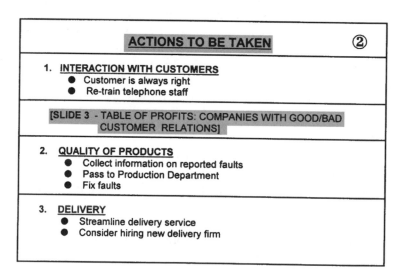

Figure 15: Cards for oral presentations

The speech should not be written out in full, word for word, on the cards. Unless someone is an actor, reading a speech out word for word usually sounds stilted and unnatural, perhaps particularly so for dyslexic readers. Of course, dyslexic people may worry that they will forget something if they do not write it all down. They may, therefore, prefer to write quite detailed notes on their cards, but they should still keep them in note form, not full sentences (for example, 'many customer complaints' rather than 'There have been many complaints recently from our customers').

It is also helpful to the speaker if the cards include reminders (in a different colour) to indicate when any visual displays, such as slides, need to be switched on and changed.

Another essential piece of preparation for formal speeches is to practise giving the speech aloud several times beforehand. This could be to friends or colleagues, or could simply be speaking it aloud to an imaginary audience or on to a tape recorder. Practising will reveal the difficult parts of the speech – the places where the dyslexic speaker may become confused or have difficulty finding the appropriate words, and will give time to get it right. With each practice, speakers will become more and more familiar with their talk, and gain confidence as they do. The practice will also help them to get the timing right: formal speeches usually have clearly set 'time slots'.

Formal meetings

For formal meetings, the preparation should include reading the agenda and all the meeting papers before the meeting. Being familiar with the subjects that will be discussed at a meeting will help dyslexic people to keep track of the discussions. They should also make a note of any questions they want to ask, or points they want to raise, beside the appropriate agenda items.

Building confidence for speaking

Confidence (or the lack of it) can play a crucial role in oral expression, especially when someone has to take centre stage and give a formal speech, or take part in an interview. Having to do things like this can be extremely stressful, causing a build-up of anxiety and fear as the day of the speech or interview approaches.

There are many things people can do to increase their confidence and to prepare mentally for specific activities such as interviews and speech making. They include deep breathing to calm anxiety before talking; general relaxation and stress reduction techniques; and working to get rid of negative thoughts and expectations. All of these enhance confidence generally, not just in oral interactions. They are therefore covered in the next chapter on 'dealing with emotions and negative attitudes'.

As mentioned above, proper preparation also helps greatly to increase confidence. Knowing that they have thought, planned and practised before a talk, interview or discussion gives people a feeling of control, which automatically builds confidence.

Rehearsing in the mind

As part of their preparation for activities that involve speaking, dyslexic people should try rehearsing the activity in their mind. Many people find this extremely effective at building confidence before oral presentations or interactions. It involves going through the activity in the imagination, visualizing not only the success, but also all the inevitable fears and doubts, and then controlling those fears in the imagination.

> Conchita had an interview for what appeared to be the perfect job. Her dyslexia made her unsure of herself at the best of times, but her desire to get this particular job was so strong that her self-doubts seemed to multiply. In spite of having all the qualifications and experience needed for the job, she became steadily more convinced that she would fall to pieces in the interview. Her dyslexia made oral interactions difficult, and the more she thought of the interview, the more she became convinced that she would misinterpret questions and give garbled, incoherent replies. She felt so sure she would fail that she began to think about cancelling the interview to avoid the inevitable disappointment. She mentioned this to a friend, who persuaded her to try a bit of positive visualization before she threw in the towel. She had nothing to lose, so she agreed.
>
> Over the following week, Conchita went through the ordeal over and over again in her mind. She pictured herself standing outside the interview room and felt the fear and panic well up. She imagined taking deep, calming breaths and feeling better. In her mind, she stood tall, opened the door and walked into the room, looking the interviewers in the eyes. She felt another imaginary wave of panic, took more imaginary deep breaths, and saw herself smiling, greeting the interviewers and sitting down.
>
> Conchita then pictured herself focusing calmly on the first question, pausing to think, and giving a coherent reply. She felt the flood of relief. She imagined the looks of approval on the faces of the interviewers. She imagined herself not understanding a question and calmly asking for a repeat. She thought of questions they might ask, and answered them successfully in her mind.

Then she imagined answering one question awkwardly, felt the disappointment, and felt herself regaining control and carrying on. She could feel herself becoming calmer and more confident with each successive question. Finally, she pictured herself calmly leaving the interview room with the feeling that she had performed well.

With each mental rehearsal, Conchita felt more capable of tackling the real interview, and more sure that she might do it well. By the day of the interview, she felt well rehearsed. She went through the real thing just as she had done so many times in her imagination and came out feeling satisfied. When they offered her the job, her delight was all the greater for thinking how close she had come to running away.

Of course, this cannot take the place of other sorts of preparation. As well as the mental rehearsal, Conchita prepared well for her interview in other ways, thinking of likely questions and making notes of her answers; speaking the answers out loud to friends; and reading up some background material about the company she was hoping to work for.

Transactional analysis

For some dyslexic employees, even the most basic one-to-one oral interaction at work can make them feel inadequate and awkward. To help tackle this, some dyslexic employees have found that Eric Berne's work on 'transactional analysis' has been very effective in helping them to become more confident and assertive when interacting with other people (Berne, 1964).

Briefly, while observing interactions (or 'transactions') between people, Berne noticed that they behaved very differently at different times. He categorized their different behaviours into three distinct states, which he called the 'Parent', the 'Adult' and the 'Child' (correlating with Freud's superego, ego and id). Very broadly, the Child feels inferior, the Adult is in control and the Parent feels superior (though it is much more complex than that; there are negative and positive aspects of behaviour in each state. For example, the Parent can be either dominating or caring).

In any specific interaction, each person behaves, at that moment, as a Parent, an Adult or a Child. The role they adopt will vary from interaction to interaction, depending on how they feel about themselves in relation to the person or persons they are interacting with. If a person is feeling inferior or powerless in a particular interaction, for example, they would adopt the role of the Child. If they felt superior, they would be the Parent. People with generally low self-esteem might find themselves more often in the role of the Child, treating the other person like a Parent, and some dyslexic people may find themselves doing this too often. (The Child may be submissive or angry, but either way the person is feeling insecure or inferior.)

For an equal interaction in which both people feel reasonably confident, neither one looking up or down at the other, people should aim for an 'Adult-to-Adult' transaction. To encapsulate this Adult-to-Adult interaction, Harris (1973) used the phrase 'I'm OK, you're OK'. (In contrast, a Child-to-Parent transaction would be termed 'I'm *not* OK, you're OK'.) People lacking in confidence should aim to move from the latter to the former interaction. Many people find that simply repeating the phrase 'I'm OK, you're OK' to themselves before a potentially difficult interaction enables them instantly to conjure up the Adult-to-Adult behaviour, looking at the other person eye-to-eye, feeling neither better nor worse than them, and behaving with confidence and assertiveness.

The above description has been only a brief outline of just one aspect of Eric Berne's transactional analysis. If people feel this would help them at work or elsewhere, they should read the relevant books by Berne and Harris listed in the References.

Body language

Body language is very important for confidence when a person is talking. The correct body language can give an impression of confidence to the listeners and a feeling of confidence to the speaker. Dyslexic people who have problems with oral presentation are very likely to feel especially nervous, and to betray this in their body language.

A straight but relaxed posture is important, as is correct eye contact. When giving a talk or interacting with a group of people, it is important to make eye contact with all the people in the group, or all sections of the audience. While speaking, the gaze should be regularly redirected from person to person in a group, or from section to section of an audience. The hands could be free and relaxed, or could be illustrating the contents of a speech. In a formal talk, it can be useful to have cards to hold to give the hands something to do. As for movement, it may help to move around a little so as not to look rigid, but not to pace up and down like a caged animal. It is also advisable to smile at the audience from time to time, rather than looking stern or worried. (There are more examples of verbal body language in the next section.)

Speaking assertively

Body language is only one aspect of the way people conduct themselves when they speak. As well as trying to adopt positive body language, people should aim to speak in a generally assertive (rather than unassertive or aggressive) manner. Saying things in a non-assertive way will betray lack of confidence, lose listeners' respect and probably fail to get them to co-operate or to do what is being asked. Saying things aggressively is likely to alienate listeners and lose their co-operation. Dyslexic people need to check whether low self-esteem or anger is causing them to speak in either of these ways, and to aim for assertive speaking. The following lists give some examples of non-assertive, aggressive and assertive speaking. (The next chapter will include some details on assertiveness in general.)

Unassertive speaking

- Too quiet and hesitant with over-long pauses; or, in contrast, too rushed or stilted and jerky.
- Mumbling, throat-clearing, hand covering the mouth.
- Looking down and failing to make eye contact while talking.
- Sentences unfinished, or words trailing off at the end of sentences.
- Frequent 'ums' and 'ers', 'you know's and 'sort of's.
- Apologies, justifications or long rambling explanations.
- Self-critical statements such as 'I'm probably wrong, but...'; 'I'm sorry to take up your time, but...'; 'It's only my view...'.

Dyslexic people are often unsure of themselves when speaking, and many of them engage in this type of unassertive speaking. They should note the above mannerisms and keep an ear on their own speaking to catch any unassertive habits they may have acquired. It may take time and practice, as these sort of self-deprecating words and mannerisms may have become automatic and habitual. Dyslexic people might benefit from enlisting the help of friends or work colleagues to 'listen in' to their talking and point out any unassertive habits and words.

Aggressive speaking

- Too loud, emphatic or abrupt.
- Glaring at the listener while speaking.
- Too fast and clipped; no pauses.
- Accompanying speech with sharp hand gestures (e.g. pointing finger, thumping fist).
- Pacing up and down while talking.
- Standing too close to listeners, or leaning forward.
- Using aggressive phrases such as 'That's stupid'; 'You're completely wrong'.

Dyslexic people's feelings of anger, at the lack of understanding and support they so often have to face, may be justified. But expressing it in aggressive behaviour usually makes things worse. Again, they should scan the above list and try to avoid aggressive mannerisms while speaking.

Assertive speaking

- Neither too loud nor too soft.
- A steady, even pace; fluent and without hesitations.
- Tone of voice matching content of speech.
- Regular eye contact, but not a fixed glare.
- Open, relaxed facial expression, or facial expressions to fit words.
- Short pauses between sentences, but no overlong pauses.
- Use of assertive statements such as 'My view is...'; 'I'd like...'; 'What do you think of this idea?'; 'I believe...'.

The dyslexic difficulties themselves – and the lack of confidence and anxiety they cause – means that it is not easy for many dyslexic people to achieve this sort of assertive speech. But becoming aware of what to aim for and what to avoid, and practising with friends, will lead to steady improvement.

The talking itself

After preparing for talking, building up the confidence for talking, and improving the manner of talking, the next step is to think about the delivery and the content of what is said.

Pace

If speakers want to keep the attention and understanding of their listeners, among other things they need to get the pace right. Some dyslexics find it hard to get their thoughts into words at all, and their talking is punctuated with long, awkward pauses. Others find their ideas tumbling out in a rapid stream, leaving their listeners struggling to keep up.

Those who have trouble finding the words should, whenever possible, prepare especially carefully before talking, to avoid too many long pauses. They could also practise 'filling the gaps' with stalling phrases such as 'Hmm ... that question requires thought...'.

Those whose words pour out in a rapid stream need to practise speaking slowly and clearly to enable listeners to follow their speech. It also helps if they try to pause between statements. Brief pauses give listeners time to digest what has been said, and slightly longer pauses can add emphasis to a statement.

Volume

Concerning volume, there should be no great difficulty in informal discussions with colleagues, other than the advice not to shout or mumble, or cover the mouth with the hands. For a formal speech, there will usually be a microphone. If there is not, the correct volume can be achieved by looking at people in the back row and speaking to them.

The content

Precision

Brevity and clarity are important when talking, whether to a single person or a large audience. People cannot go back and 'reread' what has been said or take pauses to refresh their concentration, so they may get lost in long, rambling sentences, or in overlong monologues or speeches. Short, clear sentences are best, to avoid leaving the listeners behind. Speakers should also try to stick to the point, and not lose the thread – and the listeners with it. It can be difficult for dyslexic people to do this 'off the cuff', which is why planning is important.

Structure

As with writing, oral expression should have a clear, logical structure to help listeners follow what is being said. Speakers need to remember to announce new subjects and to use linking words and phrases. Listeners have no time to work out the logic or hunt for unannounced new subjects at the same time as listening – as dyslexic people will know all too well. (See Chapter 12 for details of announcements and linking phrases.)

People should also give some sort of 'scene-setter' or initial announcement when they begin to talk. In ordinary conversation, dyslexic people are very prone to launch into speech without announcing the subject, which can leave listeners confused. Even in routine workplace interactions, people should state briefly at the beginning what their subject and aim are. (A long piece of talking or a formal speech requires a clear introduction, summarizing what the speaker is going to cover and giving listeners a general framework of what is to come.)

First impression

To hold people's attention, it is a good idea to aim for an interesting opening sentence to a formal oral presentation, with the aim of capturing the audience's attention and whetting their appetite. And seeing that they have made a good first impression can do a great deal to boost dyslexic speakers' confidence, which will help them get through the rest of the speech more successfully.

The amount

It is difficult for listeners to assimilate too many ideas in one sitting - so it helps if the talker does not try to cover too many subjects in one go, but sticks to a few key points. Dyslexic people can find this hard to do, because their minds are often flooded with ideas, making it difficult for them to select and focus on just a few main points. This is one of the reasons why it is so important to prepare and plan before talking, to filter the flood of ideas down to several main issues.

For a formal talk, the number of issues covered is particularly important. (BBC statistics have estimated that, in a 40-minute talk, an audience will be able to remember only between three and seven points.) Each point raised should be accompanied by clear illustrations and examples to give the audience time to absorb and fully understand the idea.

Repetition

An aspect of 'formal' talking that differs from writing is the use of repetition. By reminding the listeners of what has been said, the speaker helps them to remember it. It is commonly advised that a person giving a speech should 'tell the audience what they are going to say, say it, and end by saying it again'.

Answering questions

When it comes to answering questions, speakers should take a little time to think before replying. Sometimes, dyslexic people fear that they will appear slow or stupid if they do not come up with an instant answer. But rushing into speech without thought will usually result in an incoherent and stumbling reply. In fact, it looks intelligent and thoughtful if someone pauses a little before replying (provided the pause is not too long). It gives the impression that the speaker is taking the trouble to consider and weigh up a question. In the past, it was not uncommon for men in meetings, when confronted with an awkward question, to pause, pick up their pipe, fill it with tobacco, tap it on the desk and slowly puff to light the pipe before replying. This gave them time to think, and everyone else was quite prepared to wait while they lit up. These days, this idea would not be acceptable, but it may be useful for dyslexic people to use other ways to fill the space and give them time to formulate a reply. Instead of lighting up, they could, as mentioned earlier, fill the space with a few 'stalling' comments, such as 'Hmmm ... let me think about that' or 'That's an interesting question...'. (It is important, however, not to leave very long pauses before replying, as some dyslexic people tend to do. This leaves the audience dangling awkwardly.) If the stalling comments run out, it might be best to take control by saying something like 'That will need more thought. Can I come back to you later with a detailed reply?)

Listening

Keeping track of what is being said, and remembering it, is also hard for many dyslexic people. Speech is a continuous and often rapid process, and dyslexic people can find it immensely hard to keep track of ordinary oral conversations or discussions, let alone lectures in training courses or long formal speeches. It is not easy for them to concentrate on what is being said at the same time as trying to remember what was said before.

Taking control

Given their difficulties with listening – and the fact that improving concentration and short -memory can take time – perhaps the first thing for dyslexic people to do is to take control of oral interactions. They should remind themselves that it can be hard for anyone to keep up with the spoken word, and they should muster the courage to ask for repetitions, or to ask fast talkers to slow down. They may get better co-operation if they explain about their dyslexic difficulties.

In formal meetings where notes have to be taken, it is essential to take control and ask people to repeat things that need to be noted. Many dyslexic people are hesitant to do this, not wanting their dyslexic difficulties to be 'shown up'. But the alternative is to fall hopelessly behind in the note taking. The dyslexic difficulties may have been concealed during the meeting, but they will be revealed later when the notes fail to materialize. (Most chairpersons will be happy to give repetitions if it means getting a full and accurate set of minutes after the meeting.) Again, telling the chairperson about the dyslexia may elicit greater support. It may come down to a choice between being seen as dyslexic or being seen as incompetent.

Equipment to aid listening

A formal meeting is the ideal activity for which dyslexic people might request audio equipment to record what is said. (The people at the meeting will have to be told, so that they can ask for the tape to be switched off when they want to say something 'off the minutes'.) In fact, dyslexic people might consider making their lives easier by asking to use a tape recorder in most oral interactions, such as workplace discussions, oral instructions or training courses.

If people are uncomfortable being taped, they could be asked to provide written notes as a back-up.

Improving concentration and attention while listening

It is all too common for people to lose focus in the middle of a conversation or a talk; there is even a term for this: 'tuning out'. Dyslexic people are more prone to do this than most. As well as finding it generally hard to concentrate, they often find their minds racing off on to connected thoughts and ideas while someone is talking. The following suggestions may help listeners to sustain concentration.

- Listeners should keep eye contact with the speaker. This can help to stop the mind wandering off.
- They should notice the announcements of new subjects (e.g. 'The next thing to be discussed is the budget'). These give them pointers to the main issues being discussed.
- They should also look out for the logical links (e.g. 'in addition...', 'in contrast...') to help follow the thread of the discussion.
- They should try not to think of what to reply at the same time as listening to the speaker.
- They should try not to guess what the speaker is about to say. (This is a common strategy among dyslexic people to help reading and listening, but it doesn't always work and it does divert the attention.)
- They should try not to do other things while listening, such as looking out of the window.

The above ideas will help in actual workplace interactions. It might also benefit dyslexic people to practise some simple exercises to help build up their general ability to focus and maintain concentration on the spoken word. It takes time and practice to do this, but the following exercises done regularly will help. The aim is to start with short bursts of concentration and gradually build up the duration, doing a little more each day.

1 An exercise to help build up attention span is to practise listening to simple sentences and trying to repeat them. Friends or colleagues can help by reading out each sentence slowly. The listener should close his eyes and visualize the words, and then try to repeat the sentence

word for word. (Books of quotations provide good stocks of short but interesting sentences.)

2   The next stage would be to progress to slightly longer periods of concentration, and to do the same as above with short paragraphs of text. Listeners should try to spot the key words and to visualize what the passage is about. They should then try to repeat the gist of the passage.

3   Playing concentration and memory games when watching television can help to increase the concentration span even further. The dyslexic person will need to video a short television clip, then play it back and aim to sustain concentration just for the duration of the clip (perhaps only a minute or two at first, progressing gradually on to longer and longer ones). He should aim to focus on the words, and try not to be distracted by the visual aspects of the clip. Again, he will need to enlist the help of a friend to watch the clip too, and then to ask him questions about what has been said.

4   Finally, it can help to close the eyes for five minutes, and try to focus on each surrounding sound, one by one. For example, first the traffic, then the clicking of keyboards, then what one person is saying, etc.

In general, improving oral skills is best done through interactive practice or role-playing. Dyslexic people should consider looking for training courses, or taking some initial tuition sessions to practise oral techniques. They could then ask their friends or colleagues to work with them to improve their talking and listening skills.

Chapter 16
Dealing with emotions and negative attitudes

As illustrated in Chapter 7, a dyslexic person's difficulties do not stop at reading, writing and organization. On top of these difficulties – both caused by them and compounding them – there is often a barrier of negative emotions and attitudes. These emotions can have a detrimental effect on performance that is as strong as the underlying dyslexia itself.

Any tuition or training given to dyslexic people should take this into account, and work to tackle the emotions and negative attitudes along with the underlying dyslexic difficulties. Without this, the literacy skills acquired and perfected in the relative safety of the tuition sessions can crumble and all but disappear in more stressful real-life situations.

Jake, a departmental manager in a sales department suffered from severe dyslexic difficulties, particularly with reading. His company funded tuition sessions for him, and he worked with determination to develop his word-recognition and general reading skills, making rapid progress. His particular fear was reading aloud in meetings, which he went to great lengths to avoid. He would spend hours at home before meetings learning his speeches by heart, to avoid having to read them out from cards.

Jake regularly practised reading aloud in his tuition sessions. Over time, he became quite adept at doing this, and he finally felt ready to try it out at work. He prepared clear notes for his talk, well laid out on index cards. He practised the talk in a training session the day before the meeting, and gave his tutor a very good speech.

The next morning, he took his cards to the meeting and stood up to speak – and all the skills and techniques he had learned deserted him on the spot. As he began to read, all his old fears and doubts resurfaced. The fact that he had given that very same talk almost flawlessly in the tuition session the day before meant nothing. Jake no longer believed he could do it. Anxiety at the thought of making a fool of himself engulfed him, and his mind seemed to freeze up. He got stuck in the middle of long words, misread others, and frequently lost his place. In panic, he began to guess at words, but got them wrong. He finally gave up, put down his cards, and tried to speak from memory. It was better than trying to read, but without the hours of learning the night before, his speech was disorganized and he forgot to make several important points. He came out of the meeting feeling that all his training had been a waste of time.

In fact, Jake's tuition had been fine as far as it went. It had covered all the literacy techniques and exercises, and had included role-play to practise oral presentations; but it had not dealt with the emotional and mental aspects. (Subsequently, Jake found some tuition that did include this aspect. He now reads all his speeches from cards.)

Jake's story illustrates just one way in which mental barriers can hamper performance. They must be tackled if dyslexic people are to meet their full potential. This chapter offers some guidelines on how to do this. It aims to show that, as strong an adversary as the mind can be, it can be an even stronger ally.

Anxiety and stress

Almost everyone, dyslexic or not, knows what stress and anxiety feel like and how they can hinder performance. Dyslexic people probably know this better than most. Their daily battle with their dyslexic difficulties is stressful enough in itself. On top of that, there are numerous stress-producing situations facing dyslexic people every day in a typical workplace: working while being watched; having to interact rapidly in meetings; trying to follow rushed instructions, etc. In addition, many jobs these days involve overload and pressure.

The effects on performance of stress and anxiety can be severe. Among other things, they can reduce efficiency, prevent clear thought, undermine reasoning abilities, and impair memory.

Life is difficult enough for dyslexic employees without having their performance and efficiency further impeded in these ways. It is important for them to do what they can to reduce their stress and anxiety. The ways to do this may seem deceptively simple, but the simplest things are often the most effective. Basic breathing exercises, for example, or simple visualization techniques, or just 'letting go' and not trying too hard, can make a big difference.

Relaxation

Simple relaxation exercises for the body and mind can be very effective in reducing stress and anxiety, and thereby improving work performance.

In the short term, just taking a few deep breaths at times of stress can help greatly to relax the body and calm the mind. It can be especially helpful when work begins to feel overwhelming, when memory fails, when concentration begins to flag, or just before facing a stressful situation such as going into a meeting or having a discussion with a difficult person. Many dyslexic people have found that taking deep breaths at times like these helps them immensely in their work, allowing them to reduce their feelings of anxiety and get back in control of the task they are doing.

All it entails is to sit back, perhaps close the eyes, take the mind away from the task (or the situation) and take a few slow, deep breaths in and out, focusing only on the breathing. Some people find it helps to imagine that they are breathing in a stream of energy and clarity of mind, and to feel the energizing breath filling every part of their mind and body. The out breaths can be experienced as 'sighs of relief', letting go of all the tension. It may also help to visualize the anxiety as a grey mist, and to breathe out a bit more of the mist with each breath, feeling the tension dissipating harmlessly into the air.

For longer-term, cumulative release of stress and anxiety, regular daily (or, ideally, twice-daily) relaxation or meditation exercises can work wonders for anyone's performance. Stress and anxiety build up and accumulate over time, and can become an almost habitual state of mind. Regular relaxation exercises will slowly peel away the layers of stress, and whittle away the persistent negative thoughts, making the mind and the thinking processes progressively clearer and sharper. Many dyslexic people have found that doing daily relaxation or meditation exercises has improved their efficiency in every aspect of their work. One dyslexic employee commented, 'It made me feel more intelligent – my boss and all my workmates remarked on my improved work.' This as not at all surprising: a mind filled with stress and worries cannot be as efficient as a mind that is relaxed.

There are many classes where people can learn and practise the basic techniques of relaxation or meditation; and there is a wide range of audiotapes on sale containing guided relaxation and meditation exercises. Usually, the exercises combine bodily relaxation with techniques to relax the mind. It is best to attend a class for a number of sessions initially, to be guided through the exercises, and feel at ease doing them. (A basic body and mind relaxation exercise is given in Appendix B.)

Of course, many dyslexic people may say that there is not enough time in the day to get all their work done, let alone doing relaxation exercises. However, in the same way that taking breaks leads to greater, not less output, so regular relaxation or meditation works to increase efficiency and enhance output.

Visualizations for relaxing

Another effective way of reducing stress is to use the imagination to visualize something peaceful and soothing. For example, some people find their tension and anxiety dropping away if they visualize themselves in a favourite calm and tranquil setting such as a secluded beach by the sea. There are many relaxing visual images, a few of which are described in Appendix C. But any image that makes a person feel calm and relaxed will do.

Physical exercise

Many people do not realize that physical exercise can be an excellent way to relax the mind. Going for a jog, spending a little time in the gym or playing a sport can be a way of releasing tension for those who do not fancy doing relaxation exercises or visualizations.

Not trying too hard

Trying too hard or thinking too much can cause stress and hamper efficiency. (How many people find they can perform flawlessly in front of people they have no desire to impress, yet fail dismally with people they are trying too hard to impress?)

Dyslexic people often put intense effort into their work in an attempt to make up for the dyslexic difficulties. The resultant tension can 'freeze up' their thought processes, literally making them forget what they already know. Just letting go of the struggle and letting things flow out can sometimes help.

> Phil, a dyslexic supervisor with severe spelling difficulties, had taken the time to master all the memory techniques and rules to learn spelling. Yet often, when faced with spelling a familiar word he had already learned, he would visibly tense up with the effort of trying to remember how to spell it, and would find he couldn't even begin to remember. When advised to stop 'trying' to get it right, and just to trust himself and write the word without trying to spell it correctly, he found to his amazement that most words flowed out correctly spelt. His intense effort had hindered rather than helped his memory.

As well as trying too hard, thinking and questioning too much can be equally disastrous to performance. It can cloud the mind with anxious thoughts that reduce clear thinking. Dyslexic workers sometimes become bogged down in tasks because they cannot stop questioning what they are doing or thinking of alternatives that they cannot choose between.

> Nita, a dyslexic project worker, was asked by her boss to come up with a set of proposals for a survey they were planning to do. She found that no sooner did she get an idea than she began to question it. She kept thinking, 'My boss won't like that suggestion', instead of writing it down and letting the boss decide whether or not he liked it. She also found herself thinking of several different alternatives for every proposal and spending hours of anxious indecision weighing up the alternatives. The longer she took, the more stressed and anxious she became. Because of her excessive questioning and analysis, the project was handed in very late, which did not please the boss.

Of course it is necessary to think things through – but in the end decisions have to be made or nothing will get done. Dyslexic people should aim not to confuse themselves with too much thinking and analysis, or their work may grind to a complete halt.

Familiar jobs also benefit from being done as 'automatically' as possible, without too much thought. Accomplished touch typists, for example, may begin to make mistakes if they start thinking about what their fingers are doing or whether they are hitting the right keys. Dyslexic typists are prone to do this when they are being watched, for example when someone is dictating directly to them at the keyboard.

Planning and preparation

All the above techniques are specifically aimed at stress release. However, one of the best ways to reduce stress and anxiety is to do all the other things mentioned in this book. These will automatically reduce stress, simply because they help to make the job easier.

Remembering to plan for each workplace activity, working stage by stage, taking regular breaks and setting up a good organizational system will all make work easier, less daunting and therefore less stressful. Getting help from colleagues and equipment also makes life a lot easier and less stressful for dyslexic employees.

Overall, they should remember that the more organised and prepared they are, the more relaxed they can become, and the clearer and sharper their minds will be. And dyslexic people need all the clarity of mind they can muster.

Lack of confidence and self-doubt

Gerald Ford once said: 'Whether you believe you can, or whether you believe you can't... You're right.' And all too often, dyslexic people believe 'they can't'. The years of difficulty, and of being treated by others as stupid, lead many of them to believe they will fail. Even after they have tackled their difficulties, the old negative beliefs remain, and become 'self-fulfilling prophecies'.

This low confidence hinders dyslexic people in many ways. They can find themselves unable to perform even the most basic tasks because they doubt their own ability. They expect to make mistakes, and so they do. Many dyslexic workers are afraid of applying for promotion because they do not believe they will cope; they are hesitant to ask for help because they believe this will highlight their perceived flaws; and they veer away from training courses because they 'know' they will make fools of themselves. And because of this, many highly competent dyslexic employees remain in jobs well below their capability, largely because they do not believe in their own competence.

Testing the negative thoughts

The negative thoughts and expectations that erode confidence are not only powerful, *they are often wrong*. Dyslexic workers with low self-esteem are advised to take a little time to examine the negative thoughts that underlie their lack of confidence. When these are examined calmly and rationally, many of them may turn out to be faulty.

For example, when dyslexic employees get something wrong or make a mistake at work, many of them fly instantly into damaging, self-critical thoughts that are not necessarily true. They may find themselves thinking, 'I'm dyslexic – it must be my fault again' or 'I never get things right'. The truth is that everyone gets things wrong sometimes, and the 'fault' may equally lie elsewhere, or be shared. The boss may not have explained things as well as she could, for example. The thing to do is not to leap to conclusions, but to examine the problem, put it right, and learn from any mistakes.

Other dyslexic employees might react in a more aggressive but equally irrational way. They might find themselves thinking, 'My employers don't understand my dyslexia, and they don't want to; all they do is criticize; they can't even explain a simple job clearly.' This may or may not be the case. Again, the thought should be examined for validity, and the cause of the mistake should be found and corrected without attributing blame.

The importance of examining these types of thoughts is that they often manifest themselves in counterproductive behaviour. The self-deprecating thoughts will lead people to behave as if they are totally at fault and completely incompetent. The angry thoughts will probably result in aggressive, defensive behaviour, which will serve only to antagonize the boss and reduce the chances of getting either immediate help or long-term promotion.

Dyslexic people should try to examine their underlying thoughts for any faults, and consider how the faulty thoughts are affecting their behaviour. Because thoughts can be so powerful, it is important to weed out the negative or faulty ones.

It might help if they were to ask themselves some of the following questions about their thoughts.

- *'What is the evidence that my thought is correct? Am I jumping to a conclusion?'* (For example, thinking 'My boss looks irritable: she's cross with me again', when, in fact, the boss is not cross at all, or she's cross with someone else, or she's just had a bad day.)

- *'What is the effect of thinking the way I do? Is it helping me achieve what I want, or hindering me?'*

- *'Am I thinking of myself as a total failure because I got one or two things wrong?'* (For example, thinking 'Today was a total failure: I wrote a terrible report and clashed with a customer', when the full truth was that he also wrote two quite good reports, and got on well with all the other customers.)

- *'Am I concentrating on my weaknesses and forgetting my strengths?'* (Dyslexic people would do well to focus on their strong visual, creative and problem-solving skills – things that many non-dyslexics find difficult.)

- *'Am I blaming myself when it might not be my fault, or not all my fault?'*

- *'Am I making negative predictions instead of tackling something?'* (For example, 'I know I'm going to make a mess of this', or 'I'm certain they won't like me.')

The effect on performance of faulty thoughts can be severe. If people make a habit of identifying and testing their thoughts, they will probably find themselves becoming less self-critical and more confident, which can only improve their efficiency at work.

The effect of body language on confidence

The previous chapter looked at how body language affects oral inter-actions. But people's body language also has a strong 'feedback' effect on how they feel about themselves, and thus on their confidence and their performance. As mentioned in Chapter 12, the dyslexic writer who automatically hunches his shoulders and tenses his body before writing a report will find the writing flow constricted along with the body. In contrast, relaxing the body can help the writing to flow more easily.

The following experiment should help people to feel the instant effect that body language can have on the feelings of the person doing it.

- **First**, they should stand up, and then hunch their shoulders, bow their head and look downwards, occasionally darting an upward glance with the head still down. They should notice the feelings, and the effect on their confidence, that this body language causes.

- **Then**, they should straighten up and stand upright with the shoulders up, but not tight, holding the head upright but not rigid. They should look directly ahead without staring or glaring, and relax the facial muscles. They should notice the very different feelings that this body language engenders.

The problem is that body language can be hard to change, because people are largely unaware of it. Dyslexic people may have developed their negative body language when they first began to fall behind at school, when people first began to treat them as incompetent or stupid. By adulthood, it will have become an habitual, unconscious response that saps their confidence without their knowledge. It will require a deliberate effort for them to learn about the different sorts of body language, to observe their own, and to work to drop their negative body signals and adopt more positive body language.

The following lists give examples of different types of body language and their effects. Dyslexic people could practise watching out for the negative ones in themselves and replacing them with positive ones.

Non-assertive body language

- **In the eyes**, this may take the form of a downward eye gaze and general lack of eye contact; or evasive, darting glances.
- **In the face**, it might include rapid changes of expression and a down-tilted head. There may be too much smiling or an awkward 'false' smile.

- **In the body**, a person may shrink backwards or adopt a stooped or hunched posture. The hands may be dangling awkwardly, or wringing, or covering the mouth. Body movements and walking may be fast, jerky and nervous; or they may be awkward and hesitant.

This unassertive body language sends out strong messages of uncertainty and low confidence. It does not engender respect or co-operation from others, and it makes the person doing it feel little confidence or self-respect.

Aggressive body language

- **The eyes** may be glaring or staring too fixedly.
- **In the face**, the chin may be jutting out and the jaws set; and there may be a scowl.
- **The body** may be leaning forward and the hand and arm movements may be quick and sharp (jabbing movements, pointing fingers, clenched fists). Body movements may be heavy and deliberate, and the person may pace about.

As with other types of aggressive behaviour, this type of body language tends to have a detrimental effect on interpersonal interactions and on progress at work.

Assertive body language

- **The eyes** will maintain regular, but not constant contact.
- **The facial expressions** will be honest, matching the words. They will tend to be relaxed and open, and the head will be upright.
- **The body** will be straight yet relaxed. The hands and arms will move in an easy, relaxed way, fitting the words. Movement or walking will be easy and smooth.

This type of body language will generate respect and co-operation from others, and it will help the people displaying it feel confident, competent and in control. The favourable reaction of work colleagues and others to positive body language – and the beneficial effect it can have on performance – should become apparent as it is practised.

Visualizations to increase confidence

We have seen how visualization and imagination can help with memory and with stress reduction. They can also help build confidence.

Mental rehearsing

Chapter 15 looked at how mental rehearsal can help build confidence for oral interactions, but this technique can work with many other types of activity. Life has been likened to a play without any rehearsals, but this need not be the case. People can use their imagination to rehearse difficult jobs in their mind as many times as they like before they perform them in reality. This technique has proved to be extremely effective for many people. It is particularly useful for situations that make people nervous, such as starting a new job, but it can be used for almost any workplace or other activity.

Robbie, a dyslexic salesman, needed a driving licence for a job he was applying for. He feels that the only reason he managed to pass his driving test – after several failures in the past – was because, this time, he had 'passed' it many times in his imagination before taking the actual test. In particular, he felt that the mental rehearsal helped him to conquer his self-doubt, which was the only thing that was holding him back. He knew all the actual driving skills well, and had learnt the Highway Code by heart. It was purely his nervousness and lack of confidence 'on the day' that had let him down in the past.

When he did the imaginary driving test in his mind, he focused mainly on feeling the fears and overcoming them. In his mind, he saw himself taking deep breaths to calm the initial panic, and imagined himself progressing calmly through each stage of the test, focusing only on the road ahead. He also pictured difficult situations, like stalling the car, and saw himself suppressing the panic, calmly restarting the car and continuing. It had all become second nature to him by the time he passed the test in reality.

Doing this has helped many dyslexic people to succeed in a range of different workplace and other activities. It not only helps people conquer their self-doubt and begin to think positively, but it also allows them to think through each detail of an activity and practise getting it right.

Self-image

Dyslexic people often have a rather poor self-image. And, as with negative thoughts, they tend to behave in accordance with their negative self-images. It can help their performance a lot if they do a bit of work on re-redesigning their self-image.

Roberto Assagioli, in his work on 'psychosynthesis', writes of the visualization of 'ideal models' to help people build up desired qualities (Assagioli, 1965). Dyslexic people can use this technique, and put their visual imagination to work, to build up a picture of their own 'ideal selves'. The idea is to imagine, as vividly as possible, their goal (in this case, themselves, possessing all the qualities of confidence and competence that they would like to acquire).

To do this exercise, dyslexic people should begin by thinking of all the qualities they would like to possess (such as confidence, ease of interaction, calmness, competence and clarity of mind). They should then sit comfortably, close their eyes and begin to visualize an appropriate new image of themselves. They might imagine this 'ideal self' standing in front of them. They would visualize the posture and facial expression of this version of themselves - an upright, relaxed, confident stance, the eyes open and friendly, the gaze direct and confident. The bearing and stance of this person will exude friendliness, competence and control.

It may take a little while, but once the image of this ideal version of themselves has become reasonably clear, they should then imagine themselves 'walking into the image' and becoming their ideal selves. They should begin to feel their own confidence and ability, feel their own clarity of mind, their own power and their own calm determination.

Next, they should imagine themselves (in this ideal form) performing some work activities competently and successfully. Imagining themselves in this way can help them to become more and more like that. Whenever they feel their self-confidence failing, they should bring the image of their ideal self to mind – and *become* that person.

This, and a wide range of other visualization techniques are covered in Assagioli's book, which is included in the Reference section, along with a book on Assagioli's work by Pierro Ferucci (1982).

Some other advice on increasing self-confidence

The following list includes some other things that dyslexic readers can do to help increase their confidence and thereby improve their performance at work.

1 **Don't dwell on failures**. People with low self-esteem often tend to brood over their past mistakes. This is a pointless activity because it achieves nothing positive. But worse than this, it can hamper future performance and make feelings of self-doubt even stronger. Brooding and worrying consume energy and attention. This obstructs clear thought, which inevitably has a bad effect on performance at work. Furthermore, focusing on failure will make people expect more failures.

2 **'Act' like a confident person**. We have already referred to rehearsing activities in the mind. Dyslexic people can also use their imagination to help them succeed while involved in actual workplace activities, by pretending they are acting. If they cannot suppress their doubts about their own ability, they can pretend they are someone else, and 'act the role' of a confident, competent person. Many people have found this technique remarkably effective at banishing doubts and improving performance.

3 **Quieten the 'inner critic'**. Most people will be familiar with that part of themselves that seems to watch them over their shoulders, constantly putting them down, telling them they will fail and undermining their confidence. It is important to quieten this inner critic, or it will impede performance and prevent them from taking on new challenges. It can help to build up a visual image of this inner critic (an angry animal, a malevolent gnome or a stunted version of oneself) and tell it to be quiet. It is best for people to be kind, rather than aggressive, towards this creature; it is, after all, an aspect of themselves, filled with doubts and fears. However, kindly yet firmly, the inner critic needs to be silenced to stop it eroding self-confidence and impeding performance.

4 **A quota of mistakes**. Dyslexics often forget that everyone makes mistakes, and they overreact to their own errors. It may help their confidence if they allow themselves a 'quota of mistakes', learn from them and move on to the next task without too much self-recrimination. In this way, the mistakes they make can be seen as 'teachers' rather than 'failures'.

5 **Positive affirmations** are simply positive statements, but repeating them can help greatly to increase confidence. As we have seen, dyslexic people are often very accomplished at coming up with negative statements about themselves ('I can't do that'; 'I'll never get that job done on time'; 'Everything I write is rubbish'). These statements eat into the confidence. To balance them out, people might take a little time to think of some positive affirmations to say to themselves. Simple, clear statements (such as 'I *am* intelligent'; 'I *can* cope with this task' or 'I *will* do well today') can help to turn people's expectations from negative to positive. It can help set the tone for the day if people speak these statements aloud to themselves in the mirror before going in to work, and again before they go into the workplace. They can also repeat them under their breath from time to time during the day. Eventually, they can begin to believe them, and to act accordingly.

Assertiveness

Because of their low confidence, their anger and their negative thoughts, many dyslexic people behave in unassertive or aggressive ways. These types of behaviour hold them back at work, so it is important that they try to change them.

Changing the underlying thoughts can go a long way in itself towards changing the overt behaviour that follows them, but people also need to do a bit of work on the behaviour itself. They may benefit from some assertiveness training, for which there is a range of courses available. Such training courses will provide the face-to-face interaction and role-playing that will be particularly helpful to dyslexic people, rather than having to do it all from a book.

The previous chapter looked at assertive and non-assertive verbal behaviour. This section provides a general outline of other kinds of assertive, non-assertive and aggressive behaviour, to help make readers aware of their own behaviour and its effects at work.

Non-assertiveness

Non-assertiveness manifests itself in diffident, apologetic or self-deprecating behaviour. It involves trying too much to accommodate the needs and views of others at the expense of one's own needs and views. The effects of this type of behaviour are that people are not respected, and their opinions and requests are usually ignored or disregarded. Non-assertive people therefore do not tend to get what they want because they do not push for it, and their feelings of low self-esteem increase as a result.

Aggressive behaviour

In contrast to non-aggressive behaviour, aggressive behaviour may be too 'pushy'; it can become demanding, dismissive or threatening. It often involves being contemptuous or critical towards other people (in effect, 'attacking them before they attack you'). This type of behaviour may relieve frustration in the short term, but in the long term it tends to make people disliked and isolated. They will find it harder and harder to get co-operation and support.

Assertive behaviour

Neither unassertive nor aggressive behaviour is conducive to co-operation at work. Assertive behaviour is very different. It involves people calmly standing up for themselves at the same time as listening to, and accepting, other people's needs and opinions, and being neither self-deprecating nor too demanding. This type of behaviour is likely to gain respect and co-operation from others, and it usually gets results.

If people feel they are behaving in non-assertive or aggressive ways too often, and that this behaviour is detrimental to their progress at work, they should make a serious attempt to develop more assertive behaviour. Their first experiment in assertiveness might be to ask their employers to send them on an assertiveness training course.

Anger and aggression

Dyslexic people may feel a great deal of anger, for all the reasons spelt out in Chapters 3 and 7. The trouble is that, however valid the anger is, expressing it in outwardly aggressive behaviour only makes things worse. Anger clouds the mind and all but destroys rational thought. This only makes work even more difficult for dyslexic employees. Furthermore, bosses and work colleagues feel disinclined to help angry employees. Aggressive dyslexics often fail to get promotion, even if they have tackled their underlying dyslexic difficulties, because management work requires the ability to get on well with people.

Anger, particularly justified anger, is not easy to control. Dyslexic workers who find themselves frequently in conflict with their work colleagues might consider the following suggestions.

1 **Stress control**. The relaxation techniques referred to earlier in this chapter will help to relieve the stress and frustration that can explode in outbursts of anger at work. Again, the aim is not to suppress indignation or stop people speaking out for themselves, but to stop them being overwhelmed by their anger. In fact, the release of tension clears and sharpens the mind and helps improve work efficiency.

2 **Considering the outcome**. Whenever anger threatens to manifest itself in outward aggression, it might help to pause for a moment and consider the likely outcome.

3 **Taking control**. It is also worth reminding oneself that anger is not conducive to rational thought. As such, it is a weakness rather than a strength, because it takes control of people and prevents them from thinking clearly. People should aim to take on the challenge of controlling the anger, instead of letting *it* control them.

4 **Adult to adult**. Adopting the 'adult-to-adult' attitude in interactions with colleagues (as outlined under 'Transactional analysis' in Chapter 15) can also help to control aggression. Many dyslexic people have found that thinking 'I'm OK, you're OK' tends to make them feel less

antagonistic towards people they interact with. It helps them to look people straight in the eyes instead of snarling down at them or feeling contemptuous and critical of them. As a result, the interaction is likely to be less confrontational and more fruitful.

5 **Informing people**. Finally, many dyslexic workers who have found themselves in confrontation with their bosses and work colleagues have also found that things changed dramatically once they told them about the full effects of dyslexia, including the emotional effects. As with Ben, the investment banker, whose story appeared in Chapter 10, understanding about dyslexia can make the behaviour of work colleagues change rapidly from criticism to support.

This chapter has covered a variety of different techniques to help people tackle the negative emotions and attitudes that can hamper their efficiency and impede their progress at work. Different techniques will work better for different people, and readers should try them out and select the ones that work for them.

Whatever techniques they choose, and whatever emotions they are addressing, dyslexic people need to work to get out of the 'vicious circle' of emotions and attitudes so often triggered by their dyslexia. Above all, they should remember that the mind can be a powerful force. They can choose to let this force continue to undermine their abilities, or they can choose to turn it to their advantage.

Chapter 17
Telling employers

Many people who are diagnosed as dyslexic are very hesitant to tell their employer. Some (perhaps with good reason) feel that it will make their employer begin to doubt their abilities even more ('I was worried that they would begin to distrust my every move, and lose all hope in my ability to improve my work'). Some worry that their employer will interpret their dyslexia as lack of intelligence. And others feel that their employer will not understand about dyslexia, and think they are 'just making excuses'.

Of course these sorts of reaction do happen, but it is necessary to weigh up the advantages and disadvantages. As one jaded dyslexic employee recently said, 'I thought it was better to have them seeing me as dyslexic, rather than as stupid and incompetent'.

How to tell them

If dyslexic workers decide to tell their employers about their dyslexia, the key is *how* to tell them. If they simply state the bald fact, the chances are that their employers know little about dyslexia and may well make the kind of assumptions mentioned above. It is important to *teach* employers rather than just *tell* them. What dyslexic workers need to do is to inform their employers about what dyslexia actually is, *and what it is not*. And they need to give employers advice about what they can do to help, and to point out the things they are doing that might be hindering performance.

It would be advisable to set up a proper meeting with bosses, to give sufficient time to talk things through properly. Before the meeting, dyslexic employees should collect together some information to give to their employers – for example, the facts about the symptoms of dyslexia and their effects in the workplace described in 'A good day at the office?' and in Chapter 1, and the guidelines for employers given in Chapter 18.

The effects of telling employers

In our experience, the response of the majority of employers, when told a staff member has dyslexia, is usually very positive. Often, they have been genuinely unaware of the symptoms and effects of dyslexia, and are pleased and interested to learn about them. Most go to a great deal of trouble to help their dyslexic staff once they have been properly and fully informed.

A typical example of this is the story of Ben, the city investment banker, described in Chapter 10. As soon as they discovered Ben was dyslexic, and were given information about dyslexia, his employers and colleagues almost fell over each other trying to help him. They took note of all the advice on how to help and not hinder. And their view of Ben changed almost overnight from 'an incompetent, lazy and unsociable person' to 'a person who had been misjudged and underestimated, whom they could help to release his potential'. Their change in attitude played an important part in helping Ben to overcome his dyslexic difficulties and to achieve the success he has done.

Finally, it is important to remember that the advantages of telling employers about dyslexia may be twofold. If taken positively, they can benefit not only dyslexic workers and their employers, but also dyslexic people in general, by helping to spread information and awareness about dyslexia in the workplace.

Chapter 18
Guidelines for employers

There is still a long way to go before the majority of employers know about the full range of dyslexic difficulties and understand the ways in which these can affect performance in the workplace. In fact, it is not at all uncommon for non-dyslexic people to deny the existence of dyslexia altogether, or to think it is just a problem of 'getting bs and ds back to front'.

The attitude of employers – and the degree of help and understanding they are prepared to give – can make a huge difference to the performance of dyslexic employees. The experience of Archie, a dyslexic administrator, provides a stark example of the negative effects that unsympathetic and unhelpful employers can have.

Archie's employer was a professional association, and he had to report not only to his full-time boss, but also to the members of several committees. Unfortunately for him, none of them seemed to understand or sympathize with the symptoms of dyslexia.

The boss

The workload in Archie's department was heavy, and his immediate boss was constantly overworked and often bad-tempered. She had little patience, and was frequently to be seen hovering over Archie as he worked, and asking him when the papers he was working on would be ready. Anyone with dyslexia will know how difficult it is to work efficiently while being watched. Archie always made mistakes while his boss was hovering. Frequently Archie's boss, suffering from overload herself, would suddenly drop an unexpected task on him late in the day, without warning, demanding that it needed to be done urgently. The stress that this caused (both when it actually happened and when worrying that it might happen) always hindered Archie' s efficiency and speed. (It is well proven that stress and anxiety can have a strong negative effect on all types of mental performance.)

On top of this, when giving Archie a new job, his boss was usually too rushed to give clear, detailed instructions. And she became impatient and dismissive when he asked for clarification or went back to her with questions. The poor instructions and lack of back-up support meant that, on top of his dyslexic difficulties, Archie was often not fully aware of exactly what he had been asked to do.

In effect, the boss's hovering, rushed instructions and sudden deadlines were having the opposite effect from the one she intended - her attempts to speed up Archie's work were in fact slowing it down.

The boss became more and more unhappy with Archie's performance, unaware that she was one of the factors hampering his progress. She frequently criticized his work, and was too busy to offer praise or encouragement when he did a job well. In fact, her 'reward' for a job done quickly was usually to drop another job on his plate. Her constant criticism and lack of praise caused Archie's self-esteem to plummet, which further hindered his performance. Now he was battling not only with dyslexia, but also with stress, anxiety and lack of confidence.

On top of her negative actions, Archie's boss never had the time to help him with his work, in spite of being aware that he had dyslexia. She watched him working erratically and having difficulty getting in control of jobs, yet she never stopped to advise him how to plan or to break down tasks into subgoals.

The committee members

The committee members were not much better. They rambled on rapidly and at length in meetings, impervious to Archie's difficulty in taking minutes. They often became impatient and condescending when he asked them to slow down or repeat what they'd said – and Archie soon gave up trying to control their verbal stream. As a result, the minutes he produced were usually inaccurate and missed out certain points.

In addition, the committee members took no account of the fact that Archie had several other committees to work for. They loaded him with competing tasks and complained if he didn't finish them on time. Several of the committee members were of the opinion that there was 'no such thing as dyslexia'.

There is no happy ending to this story. The lack of support and under-standing of Archie's boss and committees, their negative behaviour, and the stress and overload they imposed, finally wore Archie down, and he handed in his resignation.

Experiences like this stress how important it is that employers should learn about dyslexia and its effects in the workplace, and that they should learn how their own behaviour can exacerbate the effects of dyslexia. On the other side of the coin, they also need to learn what positive things they can do to help dyslexic employees improve their performance – to the benefit of all parties. And they need to become aware of the visual and creative talents of many dyslexic people, and to appreciate and encourage these talents.

This chapter offers some guidelines as to how employers can help – and not hinder – their dyslexic staff. Employers are also advised to learn about all the symptoms of dyslexia, and the various ways that dyslexia can affect performance in the workplace, covered in 'A good day at the office?' and in Chapter 1.

How employers can help dyslexic staff

Avoid causing stressful situations whenever possible, and work to reduce worry and anxiety

- Whenever possible, give plenty of advance notice of tasks, rather than dropping a sudden deadline on dyslexic staff.
- Offer staff guidance and support on difficult tasks (without giving the appearance of doubting their abilities).
- Try not to put pressure on staff, e.g. by watching or 'hovering', or by showing impatience. If possible, do not press them to take fast notes at meetings, to take fast dictation or to write down rushed instructions.
- Let dyslexic staff know that you are available to help them out and answer their questions. Try not to look impatient if they ask for help when you are busy. If you cannot help immediately, arrange a time to do so as soon as possible.
- Encourage them to learn relaxation techniques to help reduce their general level of stress.

Try to reduce confusion and improve concentration

- Give full, clear, careful instructions, and take time to explain things.
- Give written instructions to back up oral ones (and vice versa), and present the instructions in a good, clear layout, perhaps in the form of a flow chart. Highlight key points.
- Do not talk too fast. Dyslexic employees may find it hard to keep up.
- Encourage them to break large tasks or projects down into subsections and stages. This will reduce the confusion of facing a huge task

by turning it into a series of smaller tasks to be completed one by one. It will also increase motivation by producing a series of small subgoals to be aimed for and achieved.

- Help them to plan and prioritize their workload and to schedule their daily work.
- Encourage people to take a brief break every hour. This has been shown to improve concentration immensely, and effectively increase the overall output in a day. It is especially important for dyslexic people.
- If possible, provide a quiet, undisturbed workplace.
- Read Chapters 10 to 14 of this book (on work organization and efficiency, reading and writing) for ideas on how to guide and help dyslexic staff at work.

Provide equipment and materials to make work easier

- Provide software that converts speech into text and vice versa.
- Provide tape recorders for meetings and discussions.
- Let staff use other equipment that makes their job easier, such as voice mail and dictaphones.
- Provide the most user-friendly word processing and other computer software, and take the time to show staff how to use it, and work through it with them.
- Provide visual, creative software packages for planning, incorporating spider diagrams, flow charts, etc. (For up-to-date advice on software, see Chapter 21 on sources of information and help.)

Try to increase the self-confidence of dyslexic staff and their belief in their abilities

- Give praise and show appreciation whenever relevant.
- Show confidence in their abilities.
- Recognize and acknowledge their talents and their strengths.
- Avoid making harsh criticisms or careless remarks that could undermine their confidence.

Remember what dyslexia is – *and what it is not*

- Do not forget that dyslexia is not laziness or stupidity, and do not act as though you think it is.
- Remember that dyslexic staff find written and organizational work much harder than you do, and that they have to put a great deal more energy and concentration into it than you do.

- Let dyslexic staff know that you understand what dyslexia is, and that you want to help them.
- Encourage staff to talk to you and others about their dyslexic difficulties, rather than hide it like a guilty secret.
- Remember that behaviours such as late reports or absenteeism may result from fear, and talk this through openly – and with understanding – with staff, to try and reduce their fear.
- Also remember that reluctance to apply for promotion or training courses is usually linked with dyslexia, and try to help dyslexic staff move forward in these respects, with as much help and support as you can give.

Above all, remember that dyslexia has nothing to do with underlying potential, and that giving all the help and encouragement listed above could well release someone's creativity, motivation and intelligence – and provide you with an excellent worker you never realised you had.

Further reading

Forum Briefing Paper 6. A practical guide to employment adjustments for people with dyslexia. London: Employers' Forum on Disability (tel: 020 7403 3020).

Part 3

Further information and help

Introduction

The third, and final, part of the book includes a summary of current research into adult dyslexic difficulties, and guidance on the applicability of the Disability Discrimination Act. It also lists organisations that offer help, advice and information to dyslexic and dyspraxic people.

Chapter 19
Research digest

A brief review of current lines of research and suggestions for further reading.

Although a good deal of research has been done on children's dyslexic difficulties, there has been relatively little work on the way dyslexic difficulties manifest themselves in adulthood; and most of the work that has been done in this area has been concerned with students rather than working people. Research on dyspraxic difficulties is even more sparse.

In this chapter, we look first at hypotheses about the core deficit in dyslexia, and then summarize the findings of research studies carried out with adults.

Arguments for a short-term memory deficit in dyslexia are presented in McLoughlin et al. (1994). These authors show how deficits in a component of short-term memory, the articulatory loop, could result in impairments both in the recall of spoken and heard information and in the retrieval of phonological material from long-term memory.

Other researchers believe that the core deficit in dyslexia is poor verbal/phonological skills. Data to support this are presented in, for example, Stanovich (1988) and Snowling et al. (1997).

More specifically, it has been postulated (Rack et al., 1994) that, from an early age, children need to set up direct mappings between orthography and phonology, and that children with well-specified phonological representations are at an advantage in this process, even though they may not be consciously aware of the letter-sound relationships they are exploring. Dyslexic children are thought to have poorly specified phonological representations at the time when they come to the task of learning to read and, although they usually develop sight vocabulary, they have difficulty in generalizing their knowledge to reading novel words, and have persisting difficulties with non-word reading. It is suggested that one way of conceptualizing the difficulties is in terms of a reading system in which the mappings between orthography and phonology are not sufficiently fine-grained to allow effective generalizations.

There has been much recent interest in trying to identify genetic factors that may predispose people to dyslexia. Frith (1997) states that phonological skills underlying reading development are heritable. There is evidence from functional brain imaging that dyslexics have less left-hemisphere activation, and also less activation in regions of the brain concerned with phonology, when engaged in tasks that require phonological processing. Martin (1999) reviews recent research on the possible neural basis of dyslexia, which concentrates on three brain regions or systems: the magnocellular pathway, the planum temporale and the cerebellum.

A number of research studies with adults have looked at types of phonological tasks which might distinguish dyslexics from non-dyslexics. Summarizing the results of 12 such research papers (see Table 1), there is strong evidence that dyslexics have particular difficulty in reading non-words, being generally more inaccurate and certainly slower on this task than their non-dyslexic counterparts. There is also evidence that dyslexics have relatively low scores on tests of vocabulary, phoneme deletion and spoonerisms, but conflicting results have been found regarding tests of digit naming and repeating polysyllabic non-words.

Although there is good evidence for the hypothesis that phonological deficits lead to poor reading and spelling, there is at present insufficient evidence to support the view that dyslexia could be defined in this way. Seymour (1998) points out that in some studies performance on reading non-words did not reliably distinguish good and bad readers. Rack (1997) notes that a significant percentage of dyslexics have difficulty as much with visuo-motor as with phonological skills, and Elbro et al. (1994) point out that dyslexics also have difficulty with morphemic processing.

Coltheart and Jackson (1998) argue against using a phonological (or any type of exclusion) definition of dyslexia, suggesting instead an evaluation of a set of reading subskills against age-related norms. Finally, Nicolson and Fawcett (1995) argue against a purely phonological basis for dyslexia and posit that poor skill automatization may also be implicated.

Finally, a word on factors that affect the abilities of dyslexics to compensate for their difficulties and achieve success in their chosen walk of life. Gerber and colleagues (1992) studied highly successful adults who had specific learning disabilities and found that they were characterized by a desire to take control of their life rather than cover up their difficulties. They had a desire to succeed, were goal-oriented and were

Summary of research findings (× = deficit found)

Paper	Reading non-words	Spelling non-words	Reading compre-hension	Listening compre-hension	Phono-logical aware-ness	Phoneme deletion	Spooner-isms	Repeating non-words	Naming (picture/ digits)	Verbal memory	Semantic process-ing	Vocab-ulary	Motor skills
Bruck (1990)	×				×								
Everatt (1997)	×		×						×				
Fawcett & Nicolson (1995)					×			×	×	×			×
Felton et al. (1990)	×				×				×				
Gallagher et al. (1996)	×	×					×		×				
Gottardo et al. (1997)	×			×				×		×	×		
Gross-Glenn et al. (1990)	×												
Hanley (1997)	×				×								
Paulesu et al. (1996)	×					×	×			×			
Pennington et al. (1990)	×												
Rack (1997)										×	×		×
Snowling et al. (1997)	×				×		×			×	×	×	

able to undertake what Gerber calls 'internal reframing' of their difficulties, thereby turning them into positive experiences. The four stages of the reframing process were: recognize, accept, understand, take action. In general, too, these successful individuals were adaptable, persistent, had good coping mechanisms, and were able to adapt to their environment and to create conditions in which they could work efficiently.

Papers that give helpful research summaries are: Gallagher et al. (1996) and Snowling et al. (1997). There are also useful collections of papers in special editions of: Journal of Child Psychology and Psychiatry (1998) 3(1) and Journal of Research in Reading (1997) 20(1). A succinct summary of current hypotheses about the causes of dyslexia has recently been published by The British Psychological Society (1999).

Chapter 20
The Disability
Discrimination Act, 1995

The Disability Discrimination Act (DDA) describes a disabled person as anyone 'with a physical or mental impairment which has a substantial and long-term adverse effect upon his or her ability to carry out normal day-to-day activities'.

Does dyslexia meet these criteria? The answer is: possibly. If a person's dyslexic difficulties are only mild and do not significantly affect his job, the Act would probably not apply to him. However, if his dyslexic difficulties are severe enough to impede his efficiency in certain aspects of a job that he is, in terms of knowledge and qualifications, otherwise competent to do, then he may be covered by the Act.

If it is established that a person is disabled, then it is unlawful for an employer (who employs 15 or more people) to discriminate against that person when he is applying for a job or is in employment. Care would need to be taken that a dyslexic person was not unfairly disadvantaged in such things as filling in application forms, interviews, proficiency tests, terms of employment, promotion, transfer or training opportunities, benefits, dismissal or redundancy.

Also, the employer would be obliged to make 'reasonable adjustments' to reduce or remove any substantial disadvantage caused to a dyslexic person (as an employee or a job applicant) by any of the employment arrangements in force. Some examples of adjustments which might apply in the case of a dyslexic employee would be: his not being asked to write letters or notes, if this was not a crucial aspect of his job; allocating some of his duties to another person; giving or arranging appropriate training; modifying instructions or reference manuals; modifying procedures for testing or assessment; and modifying equipment (for example, allowing the use of pastel-coloured paper rather than white if the dyslexic difficulties had an important visual component).

The Guidance Notes to the DDA also make the point that in some cases people have ' coping strategies', which may cease to work in certain circumstances. In the case of a dyslexic, it is very usual that his work will deteriorate if he is placed under stress or asked to do things within a very short time limit. It is important to take into account, therefore, that the effects of an impairment may be evident on some occasions but not on others.

As far as informing an employer about dyslexic difficulties is concerned, this is not mandatory unless the employer specifically asks about them, for instance in an interview. However, if the difficulties are felt to be significant, it may be preferable that they are mentioned. If the difficulties are deliberately concealed when a person applies for a job, and become evident later, then the employer may not be under an obligation to make reasonable adjustments.

If a dispute arises between a dyslexic employee and his employer, and informal discussions do not resolve the problem, then a complaint can be made through the organization's grievance procedure, following, if desirable, the 'questions procedure'. This is a procedure whereby the employer is asked to complete a DDA questionnaire within three months of the complaint being made. The questionnaire gives the complainant the opportunity to ask his employer about his employment working practices and what attempts have been made to see if an adjustment is possible. The employer's answers in the questionnaire should help the complainant to decide if he needs to refer the matter to an employment tribunal or if he can settle the problem without legal action. This may be a good time for an Advisory, Conciliation and Arbitration Service (ACAS) conciliation officer to be involved; or help can be sought from the Employment Service.

If the complainant believes that a tribunal decision is wrong on a matter of law, he can apply to the Employment Appeal Tribunal, details of which will be given in the notes which are sent out with all the decisions.

Further information, help and advice about the DDA and its workings are available from a number of organizations, such as job centres, charities, trades unions, Citizens, Advice Bureaux, solicitors and the Adult Dyslexia Organisation. The Disability Employment Advisers who work in job centres will be able to give information about 'Access to Work' and job introduction schemes for people with disabilities.

There is also a wide range of information material available to anyone who is affected by the DDA from a dedicated 24-hour information line: 0345 622 633 or 0345 622 644 (calls are charged at local rates). Or write to DDA Information, Freepost MIDO 2164, Stratford-upon-Avon, CV37 9BR.

The following DDA booklets are available free from the DDA information line:

- The Disability Discrimination Act, 1995 – What everybody needs to know (DL 160).
- The Disability Discrimination Act, 1995 – What employers need to know (DL 170).
- The Disability Discrimination Act 1995 – Are you facing employment discrimination? (DL 180).
- The Disability Discrimination Act 1995 – Employment provisions - EP - The questions procedure (DL56).
- The Disability Discrimination Act 1995 – What service providers need to know (DL150).
- Definition of Disability (DL 60).
- Employment (DL 70).

Also available from the Stationery Office (previously known as HMSO) bookshops is: a Code of Practice for the Elimination of Discrimination in the Field of Employment against Disabled Persons or Persons who have had a Disability.

Chapter 21
Sources of information and help

Assessment and tuition

Adult Dyslexia and Skills Development Centre, 5 Tavistock Place, London WC1H 9SN; tel: 020 7388 8744.

Dyslexia Assessment Service (Dr S Moody), 22 Wray Crescent, London N4 3LP; tel: 020 7272 6429

Dyslexia Institute, Main Office, 133 Gresham Road, Staines TW18 2AJ; tel: 01784 463851

Dyslexia Teaching Centre, 23 Kensington Square, London W8 5HN; tel: 020 7937 2408

Dyslexia Tuition for Adults (Diana Bartlett), 20A Pymmes Green Road, London N11 1BY; tel: 020 8368 3634

Helen Arkell Dyslexia Centre, Frensham, Farnham, Surrey GU10 3BW; tel: 01252 792400

Hornsby International Dyslexia Centre, Glenshee Lodge, 261 Trinity Road, London SW18 3SN; tel: 020 8874 1844

PATOSS (RSA tutors), PO Box 10, Evesham, Worcestershire WR11 6ZW

General advice and information

Adult Dyslexia Organisation, 336 Brixton Road, London SW9 7AA. Helpline: 020 7924 9559

British Dyslexia Association, 98 London Road, Reading, Berks RG1 5AU; London helpline: 020 8788 4083; national helpline: 0990 134248 or 01189 668271; e-mail helpline info@dyslexiahelp-bda.demon.co.uk

Bromley Adult Dyslexia Tuition; tel: 020 8464 6971

Careers Advisory Service. See telephone directory for local office.

Dyslexia Advice and Resource Centre, 217 The Custard Factory, Gibb Street, Digbeth, Birmingham B9 4AA; tel: 0121 694 9944

The Dyspraxia Foundation, 8 West Alley, Hitchin, Herts SG5 1EG; tel: 01462 454986; Adult Dyspraxia Network: 020 7435 5443

Fulcrum (Dyslexia Awareness Ltd), Princess Royal Centre, 4 Church Road, Edgbaston, Birmingham B15 3TD; tel: 0121 628 9944

London Adult Dyslexia Support Group; tel: 020 8870 1407

Advice on computers

AbilityNet, PO Box 94, Warwick CV34 5WS; tel: 01926 312847; national helpline: 0800 269545

Computer Centre for People with Disabilities, University of Westminster, 72 Great Portland Street, London W1N 5AL; tel: 020 7911 5000. Contact: Dave Laycock

Computability Centre, PO Box 94, Warwick CV34 5WS; tel: 0800 269 545

Dyslexia Computer Resource Centre, Department of Psychology, University of Hull, Hull HU6 7RX; tel: 01482 465589. Contact: Dr Chris Singleton

Iansyst Training Project, The White House, 72 Fen Road, Cambridge CB4 1UN; information: 01223 420101; sales freephone: 0500 141515

Foundation for Communication for the Disabled; tel: 01483 727848 or 01684 563684

Advice for employers and employees

Disability Matters, Berkeley House, West Tytherley, Wiltshire SP5 1NF; tel: 01264 811120. Offers training courses, seminars for senior managers, videos, consultancy

Employers Forum on Disability (EFD), Nutmeg House, 60 Gainsford Street, London SE1 2NY; tel: 020 7403 3020. Promotes employment for disabled people. Produces useful briefing paper (No 6) for employers on dyslexia in the workplace

Job Centre. Advice from the Disability Employment Adviser.

Opportunities for People with Disabilities, 1 Bank Buildings, Princes Street, London WC2R 8EU; tel: 020 7726 4961. Guidance on equipment, services and training

Trades Union Congress (TUC), Congress House, Great Russell Street, London WC1B 3LS; tel: 020 7636 4030. Advice, seminars and conferences

Workable, 67-71 Goswell Road, London EC1V 7EP; tel: 020 7608 3161. Offers employers specialist information and advice about disability

Disability advice organizations

DIAL UK, Park Lodge, St. Catherine's Hospital, Tickhill Road, Doncaster DN4 8QN; tel: 01302 310123. Network of local advice centres, telephone helplines and drop-in centres

Disability on the Agenda, Freepost, Bristol BS38 7DE; tel: 0345 622633; or Freepost, London SE99 7EQ; tel: 0345 622633

Disability Law Service, 52-54 High Holborn, London WC1V 6RL; tel: 020 7831 8031

Equal Opportunities Commission; tel: 0161 833 9244

Free Representation Unit; tel: 020 7831 0692. Provides free legal representation to people on low income

Law Centres, Law Centre Federation, 18-19 Warren Street, London W1P 5DB; tel: 020 7387 8570. Provides free legal advice and representation

Low Pay Unit, Employment Rights Advice Service, 27/29 Amwell Street, London EC1R 1UN; tel: 020 7713 7616; helpline: 020 7713 7583

RADAR (The Royal Association for Disability and Rehabilitation), 12 City Forum, 250 City Road, London EC1V 8AF; tel: 020 7250 3222. Gives advice on the Disability Discrimination Act

References

Assagioli R (1965) Psychosynthesis: a manual of principles and techniques. Harmondsworth: Penguin Books.

Beech JR, Singleton CH (eds) (1997) The Psychological Assessment of Reading. London: Routledge.

Berne E (1964) Games People Play. New York: Grove Press.

British Psychological Society (1999) Literacy and Psychological Assessment. Leicester: The British Psychological Society, section 4: 27-45.

Bruck M (1990) Word recognition skills of adults with childhood diagnoses of dyslexia. Developmental Psychology 96: 439-54.

Buzan T (1982) Use Your Head. London: BBC Books.

Carpenter PA, Just MA, Shell P (1990) What one intelligence test measures: a theoretical account of the processing in the Raven Progressive Matrices Test. Psychological Review 97: 404-431.

Coltheart M, Jackson NE (1998) Defining dyslexia. Child Psychology and Psychiatry 31: 12-16.

Elbro C, Nielsen I, Petersen DK (1994) Dyslexia in adults: evidence for deficits in non-word reading and in the phonological representation of lexical items. Annals of Dyslexia 44: 205-26.

Everatt J (1997) The abilities and disabilities associated with adult developmental dyslexia. Journal of Research in Reading 20(1): 13-21.

Felton RH, Naylor CE, Wood FB (1990) Neuropsychological profile of adult dyslexics. Brain and Language 3: 485-97.

Ferrucci P (1982) What We May Be. Wellingborough, Northants: Turnstone Press.

Frith U (1995) Dyslexia: can we have a shared theoretical framework? In Hulme C, Snowling M (eds) Dyslexia: biology, cognition and intervention. London: Whurr, 1-19.

Gallagher AM, Laxon V, Armstrong E, Frith U (1996) Phonological difficulties in high-functioning dyslexics. Reading and Writing 8: 499-509.

Gerber PJ, Ginsberg R, Reiff HB (1992) Identifying alterable patterns in employment success for highly successful adults with learning disabilities. Journal of Learning Disabilities 25: 475-87.

Gottardo A, Siegel LS, Stanovich KF (1997) The assessment of adults with reading disabilities: what can we learn from experimental tasks? Journal of Research in Reading 20(1): 42-54.

Gross-Glenn K, Jallad B, Novoa L, Helgren-Lempesis V, Lubs, HA (1990) Nonsense passage reading as a diagnostic aid in the study of familial dyslexia. Reading and Writing 2(2): 161-73.

Hanley JR (1997) Reading and spelling impairments in undergraduate students with developmental dyslexia. Journal of Research in Reading 20: 22-30.

Harris TA (1973) I'm OK - You're OK. London and Sydney: Pan Books.

Kirby A (1999) What should we call children's co-ordination problems: developmental co-ordination disorder or dyspraxia? Dyslexia Review 10(3): 9-11.

Martin N (1999) The dyslexic brain: insights. The Psychologist 12(7): 358-9.

McLoughlin D, Fitzgibbon G, Young V (1994) Adult Dyslexia: assessment, counselling and training. London: Whurr.

National Working Party on Dyslexia in Higher Education: Report (1999) University of Hull.

Nicolson RI, Fawcett AJ (1995) Dyslexia is more than a phonological disability. Dyslexia 1(1): 19-36.

Ott P (1997) How to Detect and Manage Dyslexia. Oxford: Heinemann Educational.

Paulesu E, Frith U, Snowling M, Gallagher A, Morton J, Frackowiak RSJ, Frith CD (1996) Is developmental dyslexia a disconnection syndrome? Evidence from PET scanning. Brain 119: 143-57.

Pennington BF, Van Orden GC, Smith SD, Green PA, Haith MN (1990) Phonological processing skills and deficits in adult dyslexic children. Child Development 61: 1753-78.

Portwood M (1999) Developmental Dyspraxia, A Practical Manual for Parents and Professionals. London: David Fulton.

Rack JP, Snowling MJ, Olson RK (1992) The nonword reading deficit in developmental dyslexia: a review. Reading Research Quarterly 27(1): 29-53.

Rack J (1997) Issues in the assessment of developmental dyslexia in adults: theoretical and applied perspectives. Journal of Research in Reading 20: 66-76.

Rack JP, Hulme C, Snowling M, Wightman J (1994) The role of phonology in young children's learning of sight words: the direct mapping hypothesis. Journal of Experimental Child Psychology 57: 42-71.

Seymour PHK (1998) Beyond the phonological hypothesis. Child Psychology and Psychiatry Review 3(1): 22-23.

Snowling M, Nation K, Moxham P, Gallagher, A, Frith U (1997) Phonological processing skills of dyslexic students in higher education: a preliminary report. Journal of Research in Reading 20(1): 31-41.

Stanovich KE (1998) Explaining the differences between the dyslexic and the garden-variety poor reader: the phonological-core variable-difference model. Journal of Learning Disabilities 21: 590-612.

Turner M (1997) Psychological Assessment of Dyslexia. London: Whurr.

West TG (1991) In the Mind's Eye. New York: Prometheus.

Appendix A
Checklists

Dyslexia check list

Reading

Did you have difficulty in learning to read?
Do you still feel that you have difficulty in reading?
Do you easily remember the sense of what you have read?
Do you feel you take a long time to read a page of a book?
Do you read for pleasure?
Do you dislike reading long books?
Do you find it hard to learn from books?

Writing

Is your handwriting neat and readable?
Do you sometimes write letters the wrong way round?
Is your spelling poor?
Do you sometimes put letters or numbers in the wrong order?
Do you have difficulty in putting down your ideas in writing?
Do you have problems with filling in forms?
    writing a cheque?
    writing a letter?
    writing a report/essay?

Speech and comprehension

Do you get confused if you have to speak in public?
Do you find it hard to explain things to people simply and clearly?
Do you make mistakes when you say long words?
Do you 'lose the thread' of conversations or discussions?
Do you sometimes 'blank out' when engaged in a discussion?
Do you find it hard to take notes at a lecture or meeting?

Memory and concentration

Do you find it hard to remember and follow instructions?
Do you have difficulty in remembering telephone numbers?
    the times of trains or buses?
    times of appointments?
Do you find it difficult to remember messages?
    do sums in your head?
    concentrate for long periods?

Orientation

Do you find it difficult to read maps?
    find your way in a strange place?
    follow left/right instructions?
    tell the time on a clockface?
Do you find it hard to look things up in the dictionary?
    the telephone directory?
    a TV guide?

Dyspraxia checklist

Co-ordination

Do you bump into things/people and often trip over?
Do you spill and drop things often?
Do you find it difficult to do practical tasks such as cooking, DIY and typing?
Do you find it difficult to drive a car?
Do you find it difficult to ride a bike?
Do you find sports difficult, especially team and bat and ball games?

Orientation/Perception

Do you find it difficult to find your way in a strange place?
    follow left/right instructions?
    tell the time on the clock face?
    read a map?
    judge distance and space?
Are you over/under sensitive to sound?
    touch?
    smell?
    taste?

Memory and concentration

Are you generally disorganized and untidy?
Do you find it hard to remember and follow instructions?
    do sums in your head?
    concentrate for long periods?
    take messages and pass them on correctly?
    key the correct numbers on the telephone?
Do you mix up dates and times and miss appointments?
Do you often lose things and find it difficult to remember where you have put them?
Do you have problems working against a background of noise?

Speech, listening and comprehension

Do you find it difficult to explain things to people simply and clearly?
When you say a long word, do you sometimes get the sounds in the wrong order?
Do you 'lose the thread' of conversations or discussions, especially in groups?
Do you sometimes blank out when engaged in discussion?
Do you find it difficult to take notes at a lecture or meeting?
Is there a delay between hearing something and understanding it?
Do you take spoken and written words literally and find it hard to understand nuances?
Do you find it difficult to interpret body language?
Do you interrupt people often?

Organization

Do you have problems prioritizing and discriminating the essential from the inessential?
Do you operate in a muddled way generally?

Reading

Do you easily remember what you have read?
Do you lose your place when you are reading?
Do words on a page seem to 'jump about'?

Writing

Is your handwriting untidy and difficult to read?
Is your spelling poor, especially when under stress?
Do you put letters and numbers in the wrong order?
Do you have difficulty putting your ideas down on paper?
Do you have problems with filling in forms?
    writing a cheque?

writing a letter?
organizing and writing a report/essay?
proof-reading?
finishing off a piece of work?

©Mary Colley

Checklist for visual processing problems

Screening checklist for visual processing problems

Some aspects of dyslexic difficulties may be related to visual problems which are not picked up on routine eye tests. If reading regularly induces headaches or eye strain, if print seems to 'jump about' and white paper to 'glare', then it may be worth consulting an optometrist who knows about dyslexic difficulties. Solutions may include spectacles, eye exercises or colorimetry. If a coloured overlay is found to be of sustained benefit, tinted glasses may be recommended. This checklist will help to determine whether referral to an optometrist with expertise in these areas is advisable. A list of optometrists specializing in dyslexia is available from Cerium Visual Technologies, Cerium Technology Park, Appledore Road, Tenterden, Kent; tel: 01580 765211.

Have you been prescribed glasses?
Does reading make you tired?
Do you often lose your place when reading?
Do you reread or skip lines when reading?
Do you ever read words/numbers back to front?
Do you miss out words when reading?
Do you tend to misread words?
Do you use a marker or your finger to keep the place?
Are you easily distracted when reading?
Do you read for pleasure?
Do you get headaches when you read?
Do your eyes become sore or water?
Do you screw your eyes up when reading?
Do you rub or close one eye when reading?
Do you read close to the page?
Do you push the page away?
Do you prefer dim light to bright light for reading?
Does white paper (or a white board) seem to glare?
Does it all become harder the longer you read?
Does print become distorted as you read?

©Melanie Jameson

Appendix B
Basic relaxation exercise

1 Put the telephone answering machine on and pick a time when there will be no interruptions (or arrange for someone else to answer the phone and the door). This is important, as getting up suddenly in mid-exercise is not good for the body, and is likely to counteract all the good effects of the exercise.

2 Sit comfortably. (Lying down makes some people fall asleep.)

3 Close the eyes and feel the body relaxing, sinking deeply into the chair like a rag doll thrown on to a cushion.

4 Tighten all the muscles in the legs and feet, and then let them go suddenly, and feel them relax. Feel all the muscles in the legs and feet becoming softer and softer, more and more relaxed, the legs feeling lighter and lighter, until they almost feel they are floating.

5 One by one, to the same to the muscles in the hands and arms, the stomach and the chest.

6 Tighten the neck and shoulder muscles, where a lot of tension can reside. Release them and feel them going soft and loose.

7 Do the same to the jaw muscles, which are also likely to be tense. Feel the tongue resting gently in the mouth and all the face muscles soft and loose.

8 Feel the muscles around the eyes going soft and relaxed, the eyeballs resting gently in the sockets.

9 Feel the whole body, deeply relaxed, almost floating.

10 Gently turn the attention to the breathing. With each in-breath, feel peacefulness flow throughout every cell of the body. Feel a release of tension with each out-breath, like a 'sigh of relief'.

11 Just stay with the breathing for a little while, noticing its quality.

12 Thoughts will come to mind. Try not to engage them. Just let them fly by like a passing flock of birds. (If you find yourself carried away in thoughts, you should just come calmly back to the breathing whenever you notice it.)

211

13 At this point, people may choose to include a visualization exercise in the relaxation. Some of these are covered in Appendix C.

14 Gently bring the attention back to the body. Feel the chair beneath the body, and the firmness of the floor beneath the feet. Hear the surrounding sounds.

15 Gently stretch the arms, legs, shoulders and neck,

16 Slowly open the eyes and look around.

17 Take a minute or two to feel firmly back on the chair and in the room.

18 **Always come out of the relaxation slowly and gently** as described in points 14 to 17 above. **Do not** leap suddenly from deep relaxation to activity - and remember that even when they are not feeling very relaxed, people are often more deeply relaxed than they think.

Ideally, this exercise should last between 10 and 20 minutes, and should be done twice a day (e.g. early morning and evening). It is best not to do it just before going to sleep, as it tends to make the mind alert and sharp, not sleepy.

Appendix C
Visualization exercises for relaxation

These exercises may be done as part of a general relaxation exercise (as described in Appendix C). If done separately, the person should sit down, relax and close the eyes before beginning.

1   Imagine a stream of pure, sparkling, crystal-clear water flowing through the brain - in one side and out the other. Feel the purity and coolness of the water as it flows through the brain, cleansing it as it goes. Feel it washing away all the worries and fears and negative thoughts, leaving the mind fresh, clear and utterly relaxed. After a while, feel the flow of the water gradually slowing down until it forms a still, crystal-clear pool in the brain. Feel the surface of the pool becoming stiller and stiller, until its surface is like a perfect mirror.

2   Imagine the body as a factory closing down for the night. Feel all the workers leaving the factory for the night, streaming out from the tips of the fingers and toes, and from the top of the head. Imagine the machinery shutting down, leaving the factory silent and empty. Feel a deep relaxation fill the mind and body as the factory closes down and falls silent.

3   Visualize a peaceful scene, for example a leafy green forest with sunlight filtering through the trees; or a beach at night with the moonlight reflecting on the waves; or a secluded garden on a warm summer's day. Use the imagination to see and hear and feel each detail of the chosen scene: the sound of the gentle breeze blowing through the trees, rustling the leaves and blowing softly against the skin; the gentle breaking of the waves, the feel of the soft sand and the salty smell of the sea; or the scent and vivid colours of the flowers and

the softness and smell of the grass. Use the imagination to be there in the scene – sink into the soft grass, or the sand, or a bed of leaves.

4 Picture any stress and anxiety as a snarling, spitting animal. Then imagine the animal curling up and going to sleep.

Index